Internet Research Skills
How To Do Your Literature Search and Find Research Information Online

Niall Ó Dochartaigh

SAGE Publications
Los Angeles • London • New Delhi • Singapore

First published 2007

SAGE Publications Ltd
1 Oliver's Yard
55 City Road
London EC1Y 1SP

SAGE Publications Inc.
2455 Teller Road
Thousand Oaks, California 91320

SAGE Publications India Pvt Ltd
B 1/I 1 Mohan Cooperative Industrial Area
Mathura Road, Post Bag 7
New Delhi 110 044

SAGE Publications Asia-Pacific Pte Ltd
33 Pekin Street #02-01
Far East Square
Singapore 048763

British Library Cataloguing in Publication data

A catalogue record for this book is available from the British Library

ISBN 978 1 4129 1112 2
ISBN 978 1 4129 1113 9 (pbk)

Library of Congress Control Number 2006928673

Typeset by C&M Digitals (P) Ltd, Chennai, India
Printed on paper from sustainable resources
Printed in Great Britain by Athenaeum Press, Gateshead

Contents

Figures and Tables

Figures

Tables

List of Boxes

Acknowledgements

Thanks to Carol-Ann for providing good advice over many months. Míle Buíochas le Caoimhe agus Dara chomh maith. Cuirfidh mé tús leis an leabhar eile anois.

Thanks especially to Peter Murphy, Elizabeth Ball and Aogán Mulcahy who read and made comments on all or most of the draft, and to Niall Ó Murchú. Almost all of their suggestions were incorporated.

Thanks to Patrick Brindle at Sage who provided great encouragement and useful advice.

Thanks also to Su-Ming Khoo, Niall Ó Cíosáin, Bernard Ryan, Brendan Flynn and John Canavan.

1
Introduction

Why not just search Google?

Internet searching seems simple. Enter a few words about a topic into a search engine such as Google and you're sure to find something relevant fairly quickly. This is exactly the way many people use the Internet as a research resource. A search engine such as Google, Yahoo, MSNSearch or Ask.com will certainly turn up a few sources on almost any topic you can think of. It's a different matter to find the central sources, the most reliable sources and the most relevant sources.

Increased reliance on the big search engines provides a large part of the explanation for a rapid rise in student use of poor quality and unreliable sources in recent years. A 2002 survey of over 2,000 US university students found that almost three-quarters of them used the Internet to search for information more than they used the library. Only 9 per cent of students used the library more than the Internet. This heavy reliance on online sources is a cause of concern to many university lecturers and professors, who fear that students are missing out on high-quality academic sources (Jones and Madden, 2002). In a 2004 survey of over 2,300 US university professors, over 42 per cent agreed that the quality of student work had worsened with use of the Internet. Only 22 per cent thought it had improved (Jones and Johnson-Yale, 2005).

One response to these problems is to ban the use of online sources, as some academics have done. The alternative response, outlined in this book, is to develop the skills to use online sources more effectively and more critically, and to place them at the centre of the research process.

Research is not simply about finding the answer to a question. It involves learning about the main issues in a particular area and identifying the central arguments made by those on all sides of the ongoing debates. It involves getting to grips with the key works on the topic, the books and articles that set the terms of debate and help you to understand the way in which those debates have developed. It also requires you to become familiar with a range of key resources specific to your subject area, including subject-specific databases and archives, organizations, professional associations, email lists and blogs. In the process of exploring the key debates and the literature, you develop a much more focused understanding of the topic you're researching, preparing the ground for searches on more obscure aspects of your topic, and the identification of very specialized resources and collections of data and documents. The research process is not only about generating a piece of work. It is also about becoming an expert on the sources and on the literature in a specialized area whose boundaries you help to define in the course of your research. This expertise is one of the most valuable outcomes of the research process.

Who this book is aimed at

This book is intended for use as a textbook for courses on Internet research skills both at undergraduate and postgraduate level, courses that introduce students to efficient and critical use of the Internet as a research resource. It will also be of use to researchers in a wide range of areas, from media to government, to the voluntary sector, who are concerned with issues of current debate and controversy. The book assumes that the reader makes regular, if sometimes unproductive and frustrating, use of the Internet.

It will be useful to advanced undergraduates writing an extended essay or pursuing an independent research assignment for the first time, particularly if they hope to continue to postgraduate level. It is aimed particularly at postgraduate students embarking on a thesis or dissertation. It is an ideal companion to the first year of a PhD thesis when a student is writing a literature review, exploring the field and identifying major resources. The book provides focused advice on a range of tasks involved in writing a thesis or dissertation, and associated exercises.

The book will also be valuable to experienced researchers who make regular use of the Internet but who have never systematically explored the resources available in their area and have never developed systematic strategies for carrying out online research.

The exercises at the end of each chapter bring readers through the material covered in the text while allowing them the freedom to concentrate on their own area of research or special interest. By simply doing the exercises readers will work their way steadily through many of the central tasks involved in their own research project. Throughout the book the importance of taking a critical approach to sources and the need to develop a better understanding of online sources are emphasized.

The book will help all readers to identify major resources in their areas, to flexibly combine a variety of online resources in the pursuit of specific tasks, to use the big search engines more effectively and efficiently, to critically evaluate online resources, and to take much fuller advantage of the huge potential of online resources in their own research.

Understanding the Internet

The Internet is not an organized system. No one is in charge. It is not primarily a network or even a network of networks. Above all, it's a simple fact – the fact that millions of computers across the world can communicate with each other. When you click a link on your computer screen, your computer sends a message to another computer asking it to send you the file the link refers to. The other computer will understand the request and will send the file. Essentially, the Internet consists of files on other people's computers that they allow the outside world to look at. To put their information 'on the Internet' people just move a file to that part of their computer, or to another computer, that is open to the outside world.

The networks that carry your request include phone lines, satellite dishes, and cables. Such lines of communication have existed for a long time. Many of them were not built specifically to carry Internet traffic and they are not the essence of the Internet.

The Internet has existed since the 1960s. That is, computers have been able to communicate over long distances since then. When the World Wide Web came into existence in 1993 it became far easier for the wider public to take advantage of this fact. The Web is based on http, the Hyper Text Transfer Protocol, and the major innovation it introduced was hypertext, the links in web pages that link you to another web page. Embedded in every hyperlink is an Internet address, a URL. It might point you to another document on the computer you are connected to or it might point you to a document on a computer on the other side of the world. It allowed people to create very elaborate documents online for the first time, including links to other documents, to graphics, to sound and to video.

The Web is not to be confused with the information people make available on their computers. Everybody puts up his or her own information. The Web 'protocol' just means that all the machines understand each other and display documents from other machines in a standard way. Web browsers such as Safari, Netscape, Firefox or Internet Explorer are not responsible for that information. They simply provide an easy way to view it.

Summary of chapters

The early chapters in this book focus on academic books and articles online, directing users towards the best organized and the most authoritative resources available, before moving on to deal in later chapters with the open Web. Search strategies illustrated by examples in each chapter combine a variety of online resources in pursuit of a series of research tasks. These strategies bring readers from the initial exploration of their topic, through the literature search, to the identification of major sources, the development of specialized search queries and the search for primary sources of data and documentation. The wide range of online resources drawn on in these strategies emphasize the fact that the big search engines, on which many people rely entirely, provide access to only a fraction of the research resources available online.

Chapter 2 focuses on academic books online. A range of online services, including bookshops such as Amazon, electronic book services such as Net Library and search services such as Google Book Search provide new ways to access the full text of academic books. This chapter outlines strategies for combining different online resources to conduct the kind of book searches that were impossible a few years ago. It outlines the way in which 'needle in the haystack' searches can now direct you to books that you would never have been alerted to through their title or list of contents, how to use these services to identify key works in your area and how to incorporate novel resources, such as reader reviews, into your search strategies.

Chapter 3 deals primarily with academic articles. It explains how to combine the databases of abstracts, full text databases, library catalogues, Google Scholar and similar tools to make full use of the available resources. It explains the extent to which these services overlap and the ways in which they differ, explaining their comparative strengths and weaknesses. It deals too with the increased access to articles, theses, dissertations, working papers, conference papers and other kinds of academic material that have been made possible through the open access movement and the growth of institutional repositories.

Chapter 4 on subject guides is the first chapter to deal with the 'open web', a realm of chaos in comparison with the databases of academic books and articles. It seeks to build an understanding of the way in which websites are organized and to set out strategies for identifying the key online resources in your area. It explains enough about the technology to allow readers to develop a better understanding of the materials they are looking at and the context in which these materials are located.

The big keyword search engines such as Google, Yahoo, Ask.com and MSNSearch are dealt with in Chapter 5. The chapter discusses advanced search options, provides advice on analysing results, explains how and what the search engines search and provides advice on building queries. It explains how to make effective and efficient use of these search engines.

Web 2.0 is the term used to describe a new generation of online services and resources characterized in part by their interactive nature. Many of these services blur the distinction between writer and reader, producer and consumer, incorporating the contributions of viewers and readers into online services to create powerful and novel means of classifying and locating information. Chapter 6 on 'Interaction, news and multimedia' deals with these services, with news sources and with a range of visual and audio resources available online.

Chapter 7 considers government sources, archives and statistics. Perhaps the most dramatic effect of the new technologies has been to open up access to these primary sources, allowing us to search millions of pages of legislative debates, to access not only statistical reports but in many cases the raw data on which they are based as well, and to make archives much more transparent. This chapter identifies key resources for searching these primary sources and suggests strategies for approaching them.

Chapter 8 sets out detailed guidelines for evaluating and understanding online sources, providing a set of questions that can usefully be asked of any materials found online. It also provides detailed advice on citing a variety of online materials.

This book focuses primarily on English-language resources, and on multilingual resources that include the English language. In every language there will be a range of additional key resources uniquely important to those searching for resources in that language but they are beyond the scope of this book.

2
Books

Print publications online

The Internet and the printed word are sometimes discussed as though they were two distinct kinds of information, one of them unreliable and suspect, the other dependable and trustworthy. Over the past few years the distinction between the Internet and the printed word has broken down completely and it no longer makes any sense to think of them as two opposing categories. After a decade of rapid technological and economic change, the Internet is now the main medium for distributing and accessing articles from academic journals, and it is fast becoming a principal medium for distributing and accessing books. If you're looking for print publications, the best place to start is online.

Although the distinction between what is online and what is in print is breaking down, the concept of print publication continues to be important. Online documents that are also available in print form have generally gone through a set of quality control measures which have developed in the world of print publishing, measures which the bulk of purely online documents do not have to go through. Print publications are much more likely to have gone through a peer review process, whereby people with expertise in the field assess whether they are worth publishing, through an editing process in which authors are encouraged to improve their work, and through copy-editing and proof-reading processes aimed at eliminating errors. These processes are far from flawless and are the subject of much harsh and justified criticism. Print publications can be poorly written, error laden and biased just like web pages, even when they have been through peer review. Decisions on what to publish are often bound up with academic power struggles, fads and fashions and complex personal networks. The essential point here is that you have to approach any piece of writing with a critical eye, regardless of the source.

Nonetheless, print publications online constitute a distinctive genre of document that is marked out from other online materials not subject to the same quality-control processes. They constitute the most clearly organized and quality controlled sector of the online world and they remain the single most important online resource for anyone doing research in the social sciences or the humanities. When you are writing on a research topic you are expected to address the central debates and the established body of knowledge around this topic in the academic literature. For this reason alone it is important that you start your research with the online services devoted to academic books and articles.

Order and chaos

In one sense, the world of print online is the best organized and ordered part of the Internet, with texts carefully selected, catalogued, indexed and stored in elaborate databases that allow sophisticated searches. In another sense, it is the most chaotic and confusing part of the Net. These texts have such high commercial value that competing information providers offer multiple routes to overlapping but distinctive databases of these texts. The publishers who own copyright on these publications make deals with a variety of indexing services in order to publicize and sell the materials through as many avenues as possible. Thus a single journal article may be listed in dozens of different databases. To take just one example, articles from *Social History*, a journal located at the intersection between the social sciences and the humanities, are indexed in more than 20 different databases. This is further complicated by the fact that these databases often index journals from different starting points so that one database will cover a journal from 1994 while another will have coverage dating back to 1984. In addition, each database may allow slightly different kinds of search. While there is huge overlap between the databases, it is far from complete and there is no single database you can rely on for comprehensive coverage. It's necessary to search a few if you are trying to make sure you have covered everything in a specialized area. To complicate matters further, you will find that many of the same databases are made available through several different commercial products, all bundling a different selection of databases together to market an all-in-one package.

Access costs

Most of the material in most of the services dealt with below will only be available to you if your university or library pays the subscription fees. Your institution will only subscribe to a selection of the services below. Many services will recognize that you are accessing the service from a computer at your home institution and will automatically give you access via their home page if your institution is subscribed. If this is not the case, you need to check on your university or library's web pages for a link to these services.

Two developments are making life easier for those whose institutions are not subscribed to some of these massive and expensive services. In the first place, more and more databases are allowing anyone to conduct searches of the databases free of charge, while limiting access to full text to sub-scribers. As search services they are useful in their own right in identifying material. Several of these services, and a range of new services emerging to cater to the needs of individual researchers, allow you to purchase single articles, although the charges for individual academic articles remain very high. In addition some services are experimenting with other innovative pricing models which cater to the individual researcher, including the option to buy access to the full contents of a database for a set period of time, an hour or two, or a day perhaps.

Alongside this, there has recently been a significant increase in the volume of freely available academic literature and some of the services below are pri-marily devoted to distributing this free literature. Despite this, the bulk of high-quality academic literature is locked up in these subscription databases and your access will be very much determined by the amount of hard cash your institution is paying to ensure that you get access to these materials.

S Search strategy: identifying key texts through reading lists

---

The first step in a literature search is to identify some of the key texts in the area, the works that everyone writing on this area has to engage with because their arguments set the terms of the debate. Your professor or lecturer should be a good starting point for information on key texts.

Beyond this, you can also get access to lists of key works in the course syllabi and reading lists made available online by hundreds of thousands of other professors and lecturers. *Syllabus Finder* (**chnm.gmu.edu/tools/syllabi/**) allows you to do a com-bined search of over one million syllabi. Not every syllabus includes a reading list but most of them do. If you find that your research topic is the subject of an entire course, or forms a major component of a course at another university, the syllabus for that course can be extremely useful, not only in providing a specialized list of key works in the area, but also in the short summaries of topics which are often provided. These can give you a flavour of the key debates in the area.

If you wanted to do research on the sociology of food, for example, you might do a search in *Syllabus Finder* on *The Sociology of Food* by Mennell, Murcott and van

---

Syllabus Finder

Search Syllabi

About this Tool

Help

Tips & FAQ

3. Warwick: Classics and Ancient History: Modules: Essays - 18k

Google excerpt: Intro. to S. Mennell, A. Murcott, AH van Otterloo, The Sociology of Food (London, ... 1994), 199-216 also in R. Buxton ed. Oxford Readings in Greek Religion ...

4. Classics: Modules: Food and Drink in the Ancient Mediterranean - 15k

Google excerpt: Intro. to S. Mennell, A. Murcott, AH van Otterloo, The Sociology of Food (London, ... Would you answer the questions under week 1 differently after reading ...

5. GCAL Logo HTLH437 MANAGING FOOD AND CULTURE General Information ... - 7k

Google excerpt: Syllabus, Social and cultural patterns and historical issues related to food and ... Mennell, S.Murcott, A & Van Otterloo, AV(1992), The Sociology of food, ...

FIGURE 2.1   Extract from Syllabus Finder results for a search on **Mennell "Sociology of Food"**

Otterloo, a key text on the topic. A search on **Mennell "Sociology of Food"** brings back seven results, among them syllabi for courses on the 'Sociology of Food and Eating' and 'Food & Drink in the Ancient Mediterranean'. These syllabi provide a list of topics dealt with and a short list of readings.

There is a strong emphasis on history courses in Syllabus Finder however, and American syllabi predominate. Some academic disciplines are organized very differently in different countries and non-US researchers will need to find out what subject headings their area of interest comes under in the USA if they are to locate useful American reading lists.

Books and articles

Just as the distinction between print and the Internet is breaking down, so too is the distinction between book and article and paragraph. Increasingly, publishers are bundling books together into online services which organize, describe and sell access to books by chapter and by page, presenting 20 or 30 related books as a kind of advanced encyclopedia or subject-specific database. Some publishers, such as *Taylor and Francis* (**www.ebookstore.tandf.co.uk**), allow subscribers to create their own books by bundling together bits and pieces from the thousands of books they sell, choosing a chapter here and a paragraph there. Publishers such as *Oxford University Press* (**www.oup.co.uk**) now provide short abstracts describing the contents of individual chapters within books and have opened these abstracts to keyword searches by the big search engines like Google and Yahoo. In treating individual chapters as discrete texts, these services erode the distinction between article and book chapter as both become search results within the big Internet search engines. The technology tends to strip these items out of the context in which they were produced. It is important for researchers to understand that context in order to better understand the content.

Reference sources

Reference books such as dictionaries and encyclopedias are easily broken into bite-sized pieces for consumption online because they are collections of short, discrete items, related through cross-references between entries. Large numbers of specialist encyclopedias in the social sciences, which provide concise introductions to key concepts, key debates and key academic writers, are available online. Some of the entries in these reference sources provide valuable introductions to key texts in very specific areas. They provide a good introduction to unfamiliar concepts and writers as you begin your research.

Several publishers who produce a range of closely related reference sources in the social sciences have bundled these books together into online reference collections, searchable by keyword and subject. Most academic libraries should be subscribed to at least one of the services listed below. Most of these services will allow anyone to search the titles and abstracts to get a sense of what is available, but only make the full text available if your university is subscribed to the service. There is a large overlap between some of these services.

Encyclopaedia Britannica online (**Britannica.com**)   One of the best-known general encyclopedias. Some features are available free of charge.

Gale Virtual Reference Library (**www.gale.com**)   A vast collection of handbooks and encyclopedias from a large number of academic publishers, including a variety of specialized social science reference works. *Xreferplus* (**www.xreferplus.com**) is the title of one of the packages offered to libraries that want to access these sources. You can limit your search to books in your subject area.

International Encyclopedia of the Social & Behavioural Sciences (**www. sciencedirect.com/science/referenceworks/008043076**)   This massive work from Elsevier, one of the largest social science publishers, includes almost 4,000 articles and is updated annually. Anyone can browse through abstracts describing the entries, organized alphabetically, but the full text is limited to subscribers. Your institution should provide a direct link if it is subscribed.

Oxford Reference Online (**www.oxfordreference.com**)   This includes a collection of several social science encyclopedias which can be searched jointly or individually.

Routledge Reference Resources Online (**www.reference.routledge.com**) This includes a collection of social science reference books.

Wikipedia (**www.wikipedia.org**) Strictly speaking Wikipedia doesn't belong here. It has no print version. It is included here because it has become such an important academic reference source. Like the reference sources dealt with above, Wikipedia organizes material by subject and aspires to comprehensive encyclopedic coverage. Wikipedia entries can be written by anyone and altered by anyone. Although it sounds anarchic this process has seen the development of powerful, well-written and useful articles on a wide range of academic topics. It provides some invaluable introductions to key concepts, debates and thinkers in the social sciences and the humanities. Wikipedia has been rightly criticized for the fact that many readers edit entries in pursuit of their own agenda and the consequent inclusion of false material. Despite this, it has huge strengths. You would not expect to use it as a central resource for a piece of academic research, or to cite it as a reliable source, but like an encyclopedia, it generally gives you a good overview of a topic, identifies key debates and provides pointers to key sources. The disputes that rage on Wikipedia are a useful reminder that knowledge is a site of struggle and contest.

A separate service called PlaceOpedia (**www.placeopedia.com**) maps Wikipedia articles on to the locations they relate to, allowing you to browse Wikipedia geographically.

Wikipedia is at its best when it comes to obscure topics and current events that would never be covered by any encyclopedia. It is hard to imagine any other way in which information on these obscure topics can be gathered together in such a concise way and be so easy to locate. Despite Wikipedia's flaws, it is simply too valuable a resource to exclude. No encyclopedia can come close to the level of detail it provides and the dynamism of its content. Unlike the sources listed above, it's free.

Library catalogues

Worldcat

With over 60 million records from the combined library catalogues of more than 9,000 libraries worldwide, Worldcat is a central source of bibliographic information on academic books. It is expanding its capabilities to include reviews and reader commentary. The service has its weaknesses and omissions, and more sophisticated searching is possible in the catalogues of individual libraries, but it is massive. Dominated as it is by academic libraries, it deals with a very different set of books from those catalogued by online bookstores. There is much greater historical depth and it is much more heavily weighted towards academic materials. You can download references from Worldcat but in many cases they have not been entered correctly and you'll need to edit them a little after importing them to a reference management package such as *EndNote*, *Procite* or *Reference Manager*. Look for a link to Worldcat from your library's web pages or go to worldcat.org.

Through a program called *Open Worldcat*, Yahoo, Google, Google Scholar, Amazon.com and several other online services now search inside the Worldcat database. The 'library search' link on Google Scholar results will take you to Worldcat information on the book in question. In Yahoo, 'Find in a library' headings on search results indicate that the link will take you to the Worldcat catalogue.

You can perform further searches on Worldcat results via Google or Yahoo but you can search much more flexibly by searching Worldcat directly. Worldcat allows you to search by 'class descriptor' (the subject classification number for the book) and by subject, providing two ways to identify closely related books. If you do a subject search in Worldcat via Google or Yahoo, you get a page of results that contain less detail and flexibility than the results received when you search Worldcat directly. One of the greatest disadvantages of searching Worldcat via these other services is that you cannot select items from the results list to download to a reference management package.

Choose the 'Libraries Worldwide' link to identify libraries near you that contain the books you're interested in. This can help to identify a nearby library which has a particularly strong collection in your area of interest and which would be worth visiting, to pore over a large number of books in a short time rather than ordering them by Inter Library Loan. If you identify such a library, you can also go directly to its online catalogue and search by the relevant subject and classification number to identify further books that it might be useful to look at while you're there. It is also useful to do a subject search of the catalogues of universities which are home to a specialized research centre or institute in the area you're working on. They should house a large and specialized collection.

Other library catalogues

LibDex, The Library Index (**www.libdex.com**) Search by keyword or browse by country to find links to the online catalogues of academic and public libraries worldwide.

The US Library of Congress (**www.loc.gov**) The official library serving the US legislature. The advanced search allows you to go beyond the book catalogue and to search their collections of manuscripts.

The British Library (**catalogue.bl.uk**) As a copyright library the British Library is entitled to receive a copy of every book published in Britain or Ireland and consequently has a much wider collection than most. It includes specialized collections.

COPAC (**copac.ac.uk/copac**) This allows you to do a unified search of major university research libraries in Britain and Ireland, by subject and by author or title. You can also search it for journals to see which libraries hold the journals you want.

Books in Print (**www.booksinprint.com**) Not strictly speaking a catalogue, university librarians and bookshops use this comprehensive guide to books both in and out of print as an authoritative source of information when buying books. It differs from Worldcat in that its primary focus is on making it possible to buy books. It also allows you to search for audio and video. You can sign up to their alert service which will send you an email when new books matching your interests are added to the database. Select 'forthcoming' to search for books that haven't yet been published.

(S)   Search strategy: searching by subject in library catalogues

---

At the early stages of your literature search you can use online library catalogues to identify closely related books. Search for a key text in Worldcat, one that relates to your specific area of interest rather than to the broad subject area. Then choose 'class descriptors' to return a list of books catalogued under the same classification number, belonging to precisely the same area of specialization as the key text. You can also call up a list of books that have been given the same subject descriptor or relate to the same geographic area.

To search for books on gender and sexuality in Victorian Britain, for example, begin by searching Worldcat for a much-cited text, such as *City of Dreadful Delight: Narratives of Sexual Danger in Late-Victorian London* by Judith Walkowitz. The Worldcat entry for the book includes a list of subject categories. Of the half dozen categories into which the book has been placed, one of them clearly fits closely with the research topic of gender and sexuality in Victorian Britain: 'Sex role – England – History – 19th century'. There are 30 items catalogued under this heading, including 25 books. Among the first ten books are several titles that are clearly relevant, including:

(Continued)

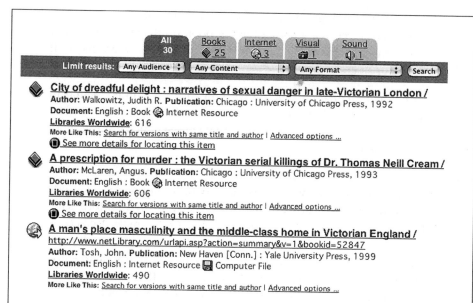

FIGURE 2.2   Worldcat results for subject category 'Sex role – England – History – 19th century'

- Limited livelihoods: gender and class in nineteenth-century England
- Banishing the beast: sexuality and the early feminists
- A man's place: masculinity and the middle-class home in Victorian England
- Gender in English society, 1650–1850: the emergence of separate spheres?

You can use the same strategy to search for books by subject in your own library catalogue.

You can also access Worldcat via Google Scholar and Yahoo. Search Google Scholar for the book (using the author surname and the first part of the title). Then click on the 'library search' link for the book. This brings you directly to the Worldcat entry for the book, including the list of subject categories. When you click on 'Sex role – History – 19th century – England' you should get a list of all the other books in Worldcat classified under this heading. But in a search repeated three times over the course of a week in 2006, it produced nothing, highlighting a problem with Google Scholar's search of Worldcat.

Yahoo describes any results it returns from Worldcat as a 'Find in a library' result and you can include that phrase as a search term to limit Yahoo results to items from Worldcat. In the example used here, search Yahoo for **'city of dreadful delight' 'find in a library'**. The link for the book brings you to the Worldcat entry you have already seen via Google, but when you click on the subject heading 'Sex role – History – 19th century – England' Yahoo brings back 55 results. It brings back more results than Worldcat because it doesn't exclude duplicates. Among the first ten results are three of the four relevant books turned up in the top ten results obtained by searching Worldcat directly and one additional useful book. While you can download the Worldcat results to a reference manager if you search Worldcat directly, you can't do this through Yahoo.

Online bookshops

Online bookshops provide powerful bibliographic searching tools as an inadvertent by-product of their efforts to sell books. Unlike library catalogues, they don't allow you to download references easily and often make it difficult to find the citation information you need. They provide an important supplement to the library catalogues in making short descriptions of books available, often including a listing of contents, and allowing us to search for books in novel ways. The online bookshops discussed below also provide significant added information on books.

Amazon.com/Amazon.co.uk Amazon has become an increasingly powerful and important source of bibliographic information over the past few years and provides several unique ways of locating books by subject. Through arrangements with a variety of other booksellers, including second-hand booksellers, it provides one of the largest bibliographic databases in existence.

'Customers who bought this item also bought' provides a unique insight into the books which other people interested in your subject area are currently buying, potentially flagging up recent publications which you weren't aware of. The option to 'Search for books by subject' presents a list of all the subject categories a book fits into. You can select some or all of these categories to get a list of very closely related books.

When you search Amazon by subject you will often be presented with a 'Listmania' column on the side, providing links to short lists of books compiled by people interested in the subject area. A large proportion of these are compiled by students. They often provide a commentary on the books, and can sometimes provide a useful guide to some of the current literature. When you select a list you will also get links to other Listmania lists on related subjects.

Amazon.com (but not Amazon.co.uk) presents you with lists of 'capitalized phrases' (CAPs) and 'statistically improbable phrases' (SIPs) which appear in the book. The SIPs are rare phrases, and many of them are likely to be uniquely associated with the subject you're interested in. They can be a useful source of very specific keywords for use in future searches. They are only provided for books with the 'Search inside this book' facility. 'Books on related topics' is a relatively new feature in Amazon.com, and is available only for books with the 'Search inside this book' feature. This will return a list of books which share SIPs with the book you're looking at.

While reader reviews on Amazon are quite uneven in quality, reviews of academic books are often quite useful because people who have gone to the trouble of accessing the academic literature on the topic generally have more than a casual interest in the topic. In addition, Amazon often links to reviews in print publications.

Amazon.com includes citation searching features, providing links to books cited in the book you're looking at and 'Books that cite this book'.

These features appear to be limited to citations in books on the Amazon database that have the 'Search inside this book' feature and therefore miss out on many citations.

The Amazon bookstores serving separate national markets have quite different collections of books and it is well worth searching both Amazon UK and Amazon in the USA for English-language books. Amazon's 'search inside this book' feature allows you to search the full text of selected books and is dealt with below along with other services providing access to the full text of books online.

Blackwell's (**www.blackwell.co.uk or bookshop.blackwell.com**)   Includes reader reviews and ratings and a 'People who bought this also bought' heading. It provides library classification numbers.

Barnes and Noble (**www.bn.com**)   This site provides short extracts from press reviews of books and allows you to search for 'more on this subject' by ticking the relevant subject classifications. They include a 'People who bought this book also bought' section.

Full-text books online

Printed books originate as computer files these days and it is a relatively simple matter to make them available online, where they can be searched much more quickly and flexibly than the printed version, and searched as part of a wider collection of books. In the past few years there has been a dramatic expansion in the availability of full-text books online, in a variety of different forms. While many of these texts, such as the reference books mentioned above, are bundled together into collections open to paying subscribers, many other texts are freely available online to varying degrees.

Amazon's 'Search inside this book' (amazon.com or amazon.co.uk)

Amazon has made arrangements with a large number of individual publishers to make the full text of their books searchable on Amazon. You can't view or print entire books, but you can view extracts surrounding your search terms, a feature with the potential to revolutionize the way in which we use books. You can also view a book's contents pages and index. The arrangements made with individual publishers determine the level of access you can get to the text around your search terms, but in many cases you can read the text of the full page your search term appears in, if you have registered (for free) as an Amazon user. Where the full text is not searchable, Amazon sometimes offers a 'Look inside this book' feature, which allows you to view the index and contents pages. In some cases

Amazon.co.uk provides full-text searching of a book not available for full text searching in Amazon.com and vice versa, emphasizing once again that it's often worth doing a search on both. While coverage is uneven and far from comprehensive, it includes many of the largest and most important academic publishers, providing access to vast numbers of high-quality, recent academic books.

By allowing us to simultaneously search the full text of hundreds of thousands of books it provides a way for us to identify books which make reference to very specific issues we are interested in. It will turn up works that you would probably never find by any other route because the book as a whole does not relate to your subject area even though it may have a useful page or two directly relevant to your research topic. It is most appropriate for 'needle in the haystack' searches at the later stages of your research rather than for general subject searches. In searching the full text of bibliographies in books it also provides a new kind of citation search. Searching for the full title of a book in Amazon, and the author surname if necessary, will yield a list of references and citations in other books, providing another way to identify texts which refer to the key works you are interested in. In Amazon.co.uk, limit your search to 'books' only, to ensure you get 'Search inside the book' results. Amazon.co.uk separates general search results from 'Search inside the book' results while Amazom.com doesn't. In some cases the exact same search in Amazon.co.uk and Amazon.com will bring up different results from a book stocked by both.

It can also be useful to carry out searches of individual books. With a copy of the book beside you, the 'Search inside the book' feature can supplement the index and contents page in the printed versions. Print indexes can sometimes be quite weak and the online search can be a valuable supplement when searching for an elusive reference in an individual book.

Unfortunately you can't yet build a collection of books which you could search jointly. If you built up a list of say 200 books relevant to a PhD research topic, it would be extremely useful to be able to limit a search to the full text of that personalized collection.

Google Book Search (books.google.com)
This service is similar in many ways to Amazon's 'Search inside this book' but has some added dimensions. Like Amazon, Google makes arrangements with individual publishers to make the full text of books searchable online. Search results in Google Book Search provide links to the books. You can view a book's table of contents and index. If a book is out of copyright, you can view the full text. In the case of most books, you can view only a few sentences around your search term, or a limited number of pages, depending on the arrangements made with individual publishers.

You have to register (for free) to view full pages. Registration allows Google to limit individuals to a small number of page views for any given book. The advanced search allows you to search by author and title and to limit your search by date. Because the content is dependent on deals with individual publishers, it is not remotely comprehensive. In addition to this, you can't easily download or copy citation details.

More revolutionary than the Google Book Search is the Google library program, which sought to bypass the publishers. Google made arrangements to scan the full text of the entire collections of three major academic libraries that between them hold a huge proportion of all the academic books ever published. Google argued that since they weren't providing users with access to the full text of these books, but only with the facility to search the full text, they weren't infringing copyright laws. In 2005 a coalition of authors and publishers brought Google to court claiming breach of copyright, bringing this Google project to a halt (BBC News, 2005; Wyatt, 2005). In the meantime Google is focusing energy on scanning books which are out of copyright. This much more modest project follows in the footsteps of one of the earliest online book projects, Project Gutenberg (**www.gutenberg.org**), which does more or less the same thing and currently has a collection of over 17,000 books.

Google Scholar (**scholar.google.com**) provides a significantly different way of searching the Google book collection. It provides information about the books which is unavailable through the Google Book Search. A result in Google Scholar labelled 'Book' (where the title is not a hyperlink) provides full citation details for the book and provides a 'Library search' link which will connect you to a Worldcat entry for the book and allow you to see if the book is held by a library near you. A result labelled 'Book' (where the title *is* a hyperlink) links you to the full text of the book in Google Book Search.

The 'cited by' link will bring up a list of sources in which the book is mentioned, including books, academic articles and a large number of pages from the open Web. The 'Web Search' link simply does a search of the open Web using author surname and part or all of the title. It brings back huge numbers of pages from booksellers who list the book for sale and is of limited use.

The link to 'Web search for reviews', which is available for some books in Google Book Search, searches the Web for the title of the book, the word 'review' and the ISBN. You can do this yourself on any search engine to search for reviews, but because Amazon reviews are mentioned on so many web pages this is of limited use and turns up masses of duplicate results.

The Amazon and Google full-text collections overlap but both services include the full text of huge numbers of books not available from the other.

Search strategy: using a key text to identify related works

A good book on your topic can be the ideal starting point for identifying other high-quality work directly relevant to your research. It is certainly a much faster and efficient way to find related work than doing keyword searches on massive databases.

First of all you need to identify a book that is central enough to your topic that many people writing on the topic feel they need to reference it. At the same time it needs to be specific enough that it is not cited by people from a wide range of disciplines.

For research on magic, demons and witchcraft in medieval Europe, for example, a good starting point might be a book such as *Europe's Inner Demons*, by Norman Cohn. While not everyone agrees with the conclusions of the author, it is a key text on the topic and a large proportion of people writing on this area are likely to reference it. At the same time your search will exclude the masses of popular literature on the topic which don't make reference to academic work like this.

This search does not need to be a marathon affair. Ten minutes should be all it takes to quickly search a service. There is no need to check out every vaguely promising looking item. If nothing looks useful at first glance simply move quickly on to another service. The basic principle is to do large numbers of quick searches using the same specific search term. No need to linger. In the example below, Amazon.com is used but the same general approach can be usefully applied to Amazon.co.uk, Google Scholar, Google Book Search and Worldcat.

After you have used a few services you are likely to find that your searches are yielding diminishing returns and I don't suggest you exhaustively mine all of these.

On the Amazon.com page for *Europe's Inner Demons,* the section on 'Customers who bought this book also bought' (seen in the image below) turns up two other books by the author which are not particularly relevant but it also turns up three others which appear to be directly relevant. Following the link to one of them, *Witchcraft and Magic in Europe: The Middle Ages*, we see that this is an edited collection, including work by a large number of authors. The fact that it comes from a university press provides another indication that it is an academic book, while a reader review mentions that it is part of a series of academic books, *Witchcraft and Magic in Europe*, that brings together historical scholarship on 'witchcraft'.

The link to the 'table of contents' for this book allows you to confirm its academic character and lists the chapters, giving you a better idea of whether some or all of them are directly relevant to your research. You can 'Search inside the book' (and browse the index of the book) to see if it contains information on very specific topics of interest to you.

(Continued)

Customers who bought this item also bought

The Pursuit of the Millennium : Revolutionary Millenarians and Mystical Anarchists of the Middle Ages (Galaxy Books) by *Norman Cohn*

Cosmos, Chaos, and the World to Come, 2nd Edition by *Norman Cohn*

The Night Battles : Witchcraft and Agrarian Cults in the Sixteenth and Seventeenth Century by *Carlo Ginzburg*

Witchcraft in Europe, 400-1700: A Documentary History (Middle Ages Series) by *Alan Charles Kors*

The Witch-Hunt in Early Modern Europe (2nd Edition) by *Brian Levack*

Explore similar items: in Books

Figure 2.3   Books bought by Amazon.com customers who bought *Europe's Inner Demons*

The section for 'Customers who bought this book also bought' on this page points in turn to several more academic books which appear to be directly relevant to the topic and which can also be explored through Amazon.com.

There is a link here to a Listmania list on 'historical witchcraft', which brings together about 20 books, the bulk of which are academic. This Listmania list in turn links to other Listmania lists with overlapping lists of academic books on witchcraft. You begin to see that four or five of the books are mentioned again and again, providing a crude indication that they are regarded as key texts.

There is little need to use the more sophisticated searching options available here because the 'Customers' list has provided more than enough to start with. If it hadn't turned up anything, your next step would be to explore some of the other options on the page for *Europe's Inner Demons*, including 'Search for books by subject', 'Books on related topics' and 'Books that cite this book'.

The sponsored links on these pages are of no use, pointing as they do to a world of magic and witchcraft merchandising which bears little relation to academic study of the topic. This is also the case with some of the Listmania lists here, which are dominated by popular books with little or no connection to the academic debates. They provide a hint of the vast store of popular materials on the subject that you have almost completely excluded from your search results simply by using a key academic text as the starting point for your search.

The result of this quick search is a list of eight to ten key academic books in the area which are directly related to your topic and whose contents you can explore if the 'Search inside the book' facility is available for those particular books. If it isn't, you can check books.google.com to see if they make the full text searchable. These books can in turn be used to lead you to other books and to articles. When you come to search the databases of journals, which is dealt with in Chapter 3, you can search for articles which cite any of perhaps three or four of these key texts. You can also use them as search terms when you are looking for material on the open Web.

In the process of doing this search you will also have become familiar with some of the core terms which are used by all of these authors, but which relate uniquely to this subject area. These can also be a useful source of search terms when you continue on to do keyword searches of the full text of articles and the open Web.

E-books

Amazon and Google allow you to search the full text of books but they don't generally provide access to the full text. E-books are online versions of books, sold by publishers. Their main advantage is that they can be purchased and used and searched much more flexibly than printed books. Publishers are increasingly bundling related books into collections and selling access to the package as a whole. Users aren't expected to read cover to cover, but to download or print a chapter here and a page there. E-books also provide novel ways to annotate and read books. You can mark important passages and add your comments. When the time comes to write your own work you can easily locate the relevant quotes.

Net Library (**www.netlibrary.com**)   Providing the full text of over 3,400 publicly accessible books, Net Library also allows you to search for e-books held by your library, if your library uses this service.

Ebrary (**www.ebrary.com**)   A subscription service providing access to the full text of over 60,000 books from over 200 publishers, The Ebrary software allows you to highlight, annotate and bookmark text. It allows you to copy and paste quotes into Word documents, automatically generating a citation. It also allows you to search other online databases of books.

Taylor and Francis (**www.ebookstore.tandf.co.uk**)   They provide several thousand of their printed books as e-books and provide a variety of ways to search and buy content from these books. Unlike many of the big online services, this service is aimed at individual users as well as institutions and is extremely flexible. The ePrint and eCopy options allow you to print and copy content for as little as a few pence or cents per page in some cases. eSubscribe allows you to buy access to material for as short a timespan as 24 hours. eCompile allows you to select content from a wide range of books, putting together a page here and a chapter there to create your own customized eBook. You can then annotate and bookmark items within the customized eBook. It's all very innovative and interesting, and has the potential to change the way we think of books as a research resource, from something you read to part of a collection you search. But all of these facilities are strictly limited in value because of the fact that they are limited to the output of one, albeit large, publisher.

When the various E-book services are finally standardized and integrated with reference management packages such as EndNote, Procite and Reference Manager (see Chapter 3) it will become a far more attractive proposition to make intensive use of E-books.

Oxford Scholarship Online (**www.oxfordscholarship.com**) This service includes several hundred academic books published by Oxford University Press and new titles are added regularly. All users can search and view book and chapter abstracts freely and these abstracts are now also searchable via Ingenta and Proquest, databases that used to be limited to academic articles. Since Ingenta is also searched by Google Scholar, you also search the Oxford Scholarship collection when you search in Google Scholar. This emphasizes the rapid multiplication of routes to any given document and the breakdown in the distinction between book chapters and journal articles. Subscribers can view the full text of the books.

Book reviews

Book reviews in journals, papers and magazines are now much more accessible and easy to search online. In addition to this, reader reviews posted to online bookshops and catalogues provide a valuable new resource, even if the quality of reviews is uneven. Some academic websites have used the Internet to distribute new kinds of book review. These are longer than normal because they don't suffer from restrictions on space, and often allow a right of reply to the reviewed author. These developments are radically altering the nature of book reviewing, by increasing the levels of debate and dialogue taking place around books.

Amazon.com/Amazon.co.uk customer reviews.   The selection of reviews on these two services overlaps, but not completely.

Books in Print (**www.booksinprint.com**)   This includes over half a million book reviews.

Book Review Index (**www.gale.com/BRIOnline**) This is a database of reviews of approximately 2 million items from around 500 journals, newspapers and magazines going back as far as 1969.

H-Review (**www.h-net.org/reviews**) This is entirely devoted to distributing reviews of academic books in the humanities and the social sciences, and is freely accessible to all. The selection is quite limited but the quality is generally high.

Publishers

Publishers like to develop concentrated expertise in specific areas. When your research is at an advanced stage you will probably be able to identify a few publishers who specialize in your areas of interest. At this stage it can be useful to sign up to their alerting services. You can generally select the subject areas you are interested in and receive regular email alerts when new books in those areas are published. Below are a few examples of publisher alerting services:

- *Blackwell E-mail Alerts* (**www.blackwellpublishing.com/ealerts**)
- *Cambridge Alerts* (**www2.cambridge.org/alerts**)
- *Sage Product Alerts* (**www.sagepub.com**)
- *Taylor and Francis eUpdates* (including Routledge) (**www.tandf.co.uk/eupdates**)
- *University of California Press Enews* (**www.ucpress.edu/books**)
- *The University of Chicago Press New Releases Notification* (**www.press.uchicago.edu/mailnotifier**)

Exercises

Exercise 1: Finding information about a book

Choose a key book related to your research topic and search for the book in at least three of the following services:

- Worldcat
- Amazon.com
- Amazon.co.uk
- Your library catalogue
- Google Book Search
- Google Scholar
- Books in Print

List the information about the book provided by each of these services (including reviews, facilities to access information on related books, and access to some or all of the book's content). You don't need to list all the citation details, just note whether they provide full citation details or whether certain citation elements are missing.

Which of these services allows you to download references?

Briefly outline the differences in the type of information provided on the book by the different services.

(Continued)

What was the most useful feature of each service?

Do any of these services provide useful information about the book that is not available in any of the other services?

Were any of the reader reviews useful? In what way?

Briefly describe the strengths and weaknesses of each service in providing information on your selected text.

Exercise 2: Finding a reading list

Search *Syllabus Finder* (**chnm.gmu.edu/tools/syllabi/**) to identify at least **three** course syllabi that provide reading lists and/or topic summaries that are directly relevant to your research topic. Note that many syllabi do not include reading lists. Search using the title and author of one or two key books in your area and one or two terms unique to your topic.

- List the titles of the relevant courses.
- Write a paragraph describing how you found the relevant syllabi, noting in particular any difficulties in locating them.
- Did you find that your topic was classified or described differently at different universities? Briefly describe any notable differences.

Exercise 3: Using a key text to identify related works

Choose a key book related to your research topic. In each of the services listed below, search for the book and then use all of the features that allow you to find related books to identify at least **three** books directly relevant to your research.

- Amazon.com
- Amazon.co.uk
- Worldcat
- Your library catalogue
- Google Book Search
- Google Scholar

List the three books identified through each service.

Write a short comparison of the three services' usefulness for identifying related books.

Exercise 4: Finding books which cite a book

Identify a key book in your research area. Use the following services to identify other books that make reference to it.

- Amazon.co.uk
- Amazon.com
- Scholar.google.com
- Books.google.com

List the books you have identified through each service.

How much overlap is there between the results returned by the different services?

Is there any difference in the results returned by Amazon.com and Amazon.co.uk?

Discuss the strengths and weaknesses of each service.

Exercise 5: Finding book reviews

Identify a key book in your research area. Gather all of the reviews of the book that you can find online, using all of the following services. If your library is not subscribed to the two subscription services, just leave them out.

- Amazon.com
- Amazon.co.uk
- Books in Print (www.booksinprint.com)
- Book Review Index (www.gale.com/BRIOnline)
- H-Review (www.h-net.org/reviews)

List the reviews, including the details of the publications they appeared in (if they were published).

Compare the relative usefulness of the various services in identifying useful reviews.

Do some reviews appear in more than one source?

3
Articles

Understanding academic articles

The development of the Internet has made academic articles much more accessible to a wider audience. They have become a central resource for students at all levels, and there has been a sharp increase in the readership of journal articles. There are difficulties with this. Journals are meant to provide a forum for cutting-edge research and many academic articles are aimed at readers with extensive background knowledge in the relevant area. Academic articles often engage with a very specific aspect of a longstanding debate and readers are in danger of missing the point of the article entirely unless they have at least an outline understanding of the key debates in the area. This doesn't mean that you shouldn't use journal articles until you've mastered your field, but it does mean that you should make sure you understand the wider debates in which these articles are located. The references in journal articles, pointing to work which authors regard as the most important work on their topic, provide a powerful resource for identifying further key books and articles in the relevant area.

Academic journals, alongside academic books, are seen as the prime location for academic or 'scholarly' debate, optimistically characterized as a kind of ongoing collective conversation in the pursuit of knowledge. Academics write for these 'peer-reviewed' journals without getting paid and the main customers for these journals are university libraries. Articles published in academic journals are subject both to editorial input and to peer review, which involves articles being assessed by those considered to be expert in the field. This level of quality control, while often criticized and far from flawless, sharply distinguishes academic articles from other kinds of publication.

The tangled maze

Academic articles are extremely accessible online but you will still face stumbling blocks. You will find it much easier to deal with these obstacles if you develop an understanding of the way in which these materials are organized. The story of academic article databases began decades before the Internet, when database companies began to store the title pages of academic journals. They allowed people to search the titles of articles and sometimes to search short descriptive abstracts too. These databases are referred to as 'indexing and abstracting databases'. They don't include the full text of articles but they remain a key research resource.

Over the past ten years virtually all of the major academic journals have made the full text of their articles available to subscribers via online databases. Some of these databases are restricted to the output of a single publisher, or of a small collection of publishers, and they are organized very differently from the indexing and abstracting databases. The full-text databases overlap with, but don't replace, the indexing and abstracting databases. It is worth using both.

The content of a database is determined by a set of commercial agreements between journals, publishers and database companies with the result that the numerous databases are a tangled maze of competing and overlapping services. The resulting overlap ensures that a single article can be listed in more than 20 different databases. At the same time the overlap is far from complete. All of the databases index material not indexed anywhere else and different databases can differ widely in their coverage of the same publication. One database may cover a journal from 2002 while

 Technical information: understanding databases

All of the information relating to a single document (author, title, publication details, abstract and perhaps the full text) go up to make the 'record' for that document. Each of these items of information is a separate 'field' in that record. Every record in the database will contain those same fields. When a record is broken into fields like this, it makes it much easier to search. You can limit your search to the author fields of all records, for example. This is exactly what you are doing when you 'Search by author' on a library catalogue or article database. As a result of this, it is possible to do a far more precise and sophisticated search on a well-structured database than it is on one of the big Internet search engines.

Search strategy: identifying key journals

When debate on a particular topic begins in a journal it may be continued there for several years. Following debates within journals can provide a much better way to identify relevant articles than carrying out repeated keyword searches in massive databases. To identify key journals in your area ask people working in related areas to recommend journals. Make a note of the journals in which key articles of interest to you have appeared and check the journals listed in your subject area in a guide such as *Intute* (**www.intute.ac.uk**, see Chapter 4). When you have identified a few key journals, quickly scan the contents pages of previous issues to identify other useful articles. Then set up contents alerts for these journals, to keep you informed of the contents of the latest issues.

another covers it back to 1994. A number of initiatives to link all of the databases together are underway and it has recently become much easier to find an article you want without checking the individual databases. Services such as Google Scholar, Crossref and SwetsWise (dealt with below) all provide different ways to search a large selection of full-text article databases simultaneously.

The linking revolution

Just as the distinction between books, chapters, articles and pages is being blurred, so too is the distinction between the different kinds of database. Indexing databases used to be a source of frustration because they provided information about articles but not the full text. Library catalogues provided information about books but couldn't tell you if they were available online, and databases of full-text articles were frustrating because many of them were limited to the output of a single publisher, ensuring that you would have to search several of them if you wanted to search all of the full-text articles available online.

We are currently in the midst of a linking revolution that is moving faster than almost anyone can keep up with. Libraries, publishers and database companies have been operating in a state of constant flux over the past ten years, but recent developments have seen the emergence of some common standards which promise to bring an end to much of the chaos and confusion for everyone involved.

One result of this linking revolution is that the distinction between a database that provides full text, a database that simply stores titles and abstracts of articles, and a library that simply catalogues the details of the journals it is subscribed to, is collapsing. These three alternative routes to journal articles are being linked seamlessly together and the emerging standards are transforming the routes by which we can move from one database and from one print publication to another. The end result is that we can reach the full text of an article almost as quickly through a library or an indexing database as we can through a full-text database.

The key to this shift is OpenURL links. These links make it easy to flick from one document to another regardless of which database they're hosted in. Popular manifestations of OpenURL linking include SFX and MetaLib. In all sorts of databases you will now see an SFX or MetaLib or similar link beside the titles of articles or books retrieved in your search results. The link takes you directly to the item in question or to your own institution's records on this article or book, allowing you to easily access the online copies that your institution has access to. It renders irrelevant the distinction between a full-text database and an indexing database because both of them can now lead you quickly to the full text. OpenURL linking is being increasingly used within articles in full-text databases to provide links to cited references. This makes it a much simpler matter to chase up references and makes academic articles much more like web pages, providing lots of hyperlinks to the full text of related documents. One of the frustrations of OpenURL linking is that it often reveals that your own library does not provide access to the article in question simply because it does not have a subscription to the journal.

Managing references

Virtually every online database of articles and every online library catalogue allows you to download and import references into reference management software. Packages such as EndNote, Reference Manager and Procite provide a way to organize and store bibliographical references. You can then generate bibliographies automatically and insert references easily into your documents. If you need to change the references in a document to a different citation format you can do it with a click of the mouse. These packages can all be used in tandem with the popular word processing packages Microsoft Word and WordPerfect.

This software requires a significant initial investment in time and many of the packages can be a little inflexible. Having said that, the initial investment in time is well worth making for anyone embarking on a major research project such as an MA or PhD thesis, or for anyone planning to be involved in research over a period of a few years.

There are many guides to reference management software available online, often provided by university libraries. A search on the name of the package you're using and a term such as **tutorial** or **guide** will bring back several useful guides.

The next step for reference management software is to integrate bibliographical references more fully with the full text of articles and academic books. This is already happening in the sciences. For example, QUOSA, a package popular with medical scientists, allows users to download the full text of articles from selected databases alongside the bibliographical references, storing both together in a reference management package. It then allows the user to highlight passages from the articles and to jointly search the downloaded articles. The result is a very specialized, searchable personal library. The software also has collaborative features, allowing a team of researchers to build up a joint annotated library on their specialized topic. It seems only a matter of time before these capabilities are available in popular packages aimed at the social sciences and humanities.

CrossRef

Involving over 1,400 academic publishers and associations, CrossRef allows joint searching of the full text of academic journal articles available online from a wide variety of publishers. It was a precursor to Google Scholar but it provides a more focused and restrictive search than Google Scholar does. Many databases that provide full text do not actually allow you to search the full text of articles but CrossRef does. CrossRef searching is available as a search option on the sites of participating publishers, such as Sage (**sagepub.com**) Blackwell (**www.blackwell-synergy.com**) and Cambridge (**journals.cambridge.org**). Links lead you to the full text of articles if your institution is a subscriber and to the abstracts if it is not. Several of the databases participating in CrossRef also provide conference proceedings, book chapters, books and encyclopaedia entries. Google provides the technology for the CrossRef search, and with the emergence of Google Scholar, CrossRef has faded into the shadows. It is more tightly limited to the output of academic publishers than Google Scholar is and remains a useful resource.

CrossRef allows the references in an article to be presented as hyperlinks, linking the reader directly to the full text of a cited article, even if it's on another publisher's database. CrossRef doesn't replace existing services. It simply links them together in a uniquely powerful way.

Annual Reviews (arjournals. annualreviews.org)

The annual reviews deal with several social science disciplines, including anthropology, environment and resources, law and social science, political science, psychology, public health and sociology. Articles in the reviews survey academic work on a particular topic, reviewing the debates and discussing significant recent work on the topic. They are among the most widely read academic articles because they provide a guide to the existing literature. You can limit your search to one review or search them jointly. You can search the titles and keywords of review articles using broad search terms to see if an article has been devoted to your research area. You can also effectively search for an article by searching the full text for a reference to the subject matter or to a key text on the topic and the surname of a key writer in the area. For example, a search on "**sociology of food**" brings up a 2002 review article on 'The Anthropology of Food and Eating'. The reviews can provide a useful way to learn about current debate in your area of research but note that many articles are pitched at a high level, aimed at describing the state of play in the field to those with a good grounding in the topic. You can also search these reviews through CrossRef and Google Scholar.

Google Scholar (Scholar.google.com)

The popularity and simplicity of Google has ensured that Google Scholar has rapidly become one of the most popular ways to search for academic articles and books. This has provoked a backlash from some, who point out that it is far less comprehensive and less clearly structured than established academic databases. The critics are right. Google Scholar is severely flawed and doesn't stand up to comparison with the established academic databases (see Jacso, 2005, for example). The enthusiastic adopters of Google Scholar are also right, however. It provides a fast, simple way to access the academic literature without learning about lots of different databases. It's on the open web, it's easy to use and it's free, although more often than not it guides you to articles that are not freely available to the public. If you're simply looking for the full text of an article whose title and author you know, Google Scholar is unquestionably the best place to start your search. If you want to find an academic article on a very specific subject Google Scholar is more useful than ordinary Google because it limits your search to academic materials. It has the advantage over the big abstracting and indexing databases in that it searches the full text of collections rather than just the abstracts and keywords. The only alternative way of simultaneously searching the full text of academic articles from the databases of multiple publishers is through a CrossRef search (discussed above).

Among the full-text collections and databases searched by Google Scholar are Taylor and Francis, CSA, JSTOR, Ingenta Connect and Project Muse, all of them described in more detail below. These full-text databases used to be regarded as part of the 'Invisible Web' or the 'Deep Web', because the content was inaccessible to search engines. Google Scholar doesn't search all of the full-text databases, however, and it doesn't allow the kind of sophisticated searching that is possible if you search the databases themselves directly. Google Scholar only seems to search a fraction of the materials on these sites (Jacso, 2005). You will get far more results if you search on the sites directly. Google Scholar also searches a variety of open access repositories (see below) and a range of other materials from the open web that Google classifies as 'scholarly' or academic, including materials from academic publisher websites and university websites. As such it is far broader than the article databases. This is useful if your search isn't bringing back enough results, but not so useful if you're already bringing back too many. Google Scholar is best used in tandem with the indexing and abstracting databases and the full-text databases rather than as a substitute. The other databases are better organized, more tightly limited to academic articles and books, and can be searched in a more sophisticated way than Google Scholar. The 'cited by' feature in Google Scholar, for example, is very crude compared to the citation searches possible in ISI Web of Science and Scopus. You will miss a lot if you rely entirely on Google Scholar. To facilitate the downloading of references from Google Scholar, select 'Scholar preferences' and choose your preferred reference management package from the 'Bibliography Manager' section.

Each Google Scholar result includes a 'Cited by' link to documents that cite the article or book concerned and a 'Web Search' link that will carry out a search on Google using elements from the title and author name. In the UK and Ireland the 'BL Direct' link connects you to the British Library's ordering service, allowing you to buy a copy of the article. If you have chosen a reference management package, there will be a link allowing you to import the reference.

In many cases a result will be part of a 'group of 2' (or more). This link will show you the various versions of the article available online. Open access articles in particular can often be available in multiple versions at many locations.

Entries for books have a slightly different set of links. The 'more info in...' link will link you to information about availability of the item via your own institution. The 'Library search' link will bring you to the Worldcat entry for the book, showing you a list of nearby libraries where the book is available.

BETA | `"the art of memory"` | (Search) | Advanced Scholar Search
Scholar Preferences
Scholar Help

The following words are very common and were not included in your search: **the of**.
[details]

Scholar   Results 1 - **10** of about **399,000** for the <u>art</u> of <u>memory</u>. (0.08 seconds)

All articles Recent articles

[BOOK] The **art** of **memory**
FA Yates - 1974 - University of Chicago Press Chicago
<u>Cited by 341</u> - <u>Web Search</u> - <u>Import into EndNote</u> - <u>Library Search</u>

[BOOK] History As an **Art** of **Memory**
PH Hutton - 1993 - books.google.com
... I began with the book by Frances Yates on the revival of the **art** of **memory** during
the Re- naissance. ... It was here that I returned to the **art** of **memory** as ...
<u>Cited by 52</u> - <u>Web Search</u> - <u>Import into EndNote</u> - <u>Library Search</u>

Malangan: **Art** and **Memory** in a Melanesian Society
S Kuchler - Man, 1987 - JSTOR
.page { padding: 1em; } Malangan: **Art** and **Memory** in a Melanesian Society. Susanne
Kuchler. Man, New Series, Vol. ... The **art** of **memory** is like an inner writing. ...
<u>Cited by 15</u> - <u>Web Search</u> - <u>Import into EndNote</u>

FIGURE 3.1   Google Scholar search results

Because there are now so many different routes to a single item, you may
find that several of the links Google Scholar provides to an article all lead you
to the same source. One of the biggest difficulties is the amount of redundant
results it brings up, often returning multiple references to a single item
(Jacso, 2005). In the advanced search you can restrict your search by subject
area and date. You can also search on author, publication and title.

    Search tip: accessing an article from a journal
your institution is not subscribed to

You will often find that your institution is not subscribed to the online version of a journal in which you've located a vital article. In all likelihood you will have to order it by
inter-library loan or pay a fee to get an electronic copy of the article, but it's worth trying a few other routes first.

1   Search Google Scholar on the title and author to see if this points you to a free
copy of the article. Google Scholar points to multiple versions of the same article
and will often turn up a version of an article that was originally delivered as a conference paper or published as a working paper and is freely available online. It
may not be the exact same text but it will still be useful.

(Continued)

2 If the article is more than three years old and your institution is subscribed to JSTOR, search for it there. You may have access to back issues through JSTOR even if you can't access current issues and Google Scholar may have missed it.

3 Locate a home page for the author by searching for the name of the author and his or her university on Google, Yahoo, MSNSearch or Ask.com. The author might provide a link to the full text of a version of this paper or to closely related work that might be equally useful.

4 Search an Open Access search engine such as *OAIster* (**oaister.umdl. umich.edu/o/oaister**) to see if a version of the paper has been made freely available in an open access archive.

5 Search your own library catalogue to see if the library subscribes to the print version of the journal.

6 If the journal is not included in any of the full-text databases, it may have a website through which it make articles freely available on the open Web. This is particularly relevant for minor journals.

If you need to get a large number of articles from a journal your institution doesn't subscribe to, locate an article from the journal in OCLC ArticleFirst and select 'libraries worldwide' to see if a nearby library holds the journal. If so, it might be worthwhile trying to arrange to get access to the journal there.

Windows Live Academic

When Windows Live Academic (**academic.live.com**) launched in beta form in 2006 it was limited to sources in computer science, physics and electrical engineering. The service's coverage is set to expand to cover a much wider range of subjects, including the social sciences and the humanities. It is a very powerful and sophisticated free service that could easily become a major rival to Google Scholar. It includes Open Access repositories.

Indexing and abstracting databases

Indexing and abstracting databases provide citation details such as author, title, year and place of publication. They also include keywords (five or six words chosen by the author of an article to describe its subject area) and abstracts (short pieces of text describing the contents of an article). The indexing services originated with the first attempts to make information about articles available in searchable form, long before full-text availability online had been dreamt of. Because they are not concerned with whether a journal is available online in full text, they are much more comprehensive than the full-text services. They include articles from large numbers of journals that are not available in any of the full-text services. Users often found it frustrating in the past that these databases delivered information about articles but not the full text. OpenURL links now allow these databases to provide links to the full text of articles. In addition to that, some of these indexing services have begun to add large full-text collections, further breaking down the distinctions between these databases and the full-text databases.

A few big services attempt to be universal, to comprehensively cover all of the social sciences. The overlap in content between these services is huge but far from complete, and it is always worth trying a few of them. In most cases below, URLs are not provided because you will need to follow a link from your own library or university's website in order to gain access. All of these services allow you to download references and import them into software such as EndNote and Reference Manager.

OCLC ArticleFirst

This massive service indexes over 22,000 journals and other periodicals in the social sciences, humanities and popular culture and includes over 19 million records. It includes current affairs magazines and reviews of books. Unlike many of the other databases listed here, it does not provide abstracts of articles and therefore allows a much more limited search of the articles than is possible in those databases.

One of the weaknesses of OCLC ArticleFirst is the fact that it has no subject search and no option to search for articles related to the article you're looking at. You can browse or search their list of journal titles to see if they index the journals of most interest to you. You can limit your search to an individual journal. You can also limit your search to items which your library subscribes to and which you will therefore have access to, saving the frustration of turning up a large list of results which you can't access. Through an OpenURL link such as SFX or MetaLib you can connect to your own library's records in relation to this article, which should link you directly to the full text of the article if your library has access to it. ArticleFirst provides the unique service of listing libraries that hold the journal in question.

ISI Web of Science (isiknowledge.com)

ISI Web of Science includes the *Social Sciences Citation Index* and the *Arts and Humanities Citation Index*. They can be searched separately or jointly.

FIGURE 3.2   OCLC ArticleFirst Basic Search

It is the original academic citation database. Like all of the other services dealt with here, it is certainly not comprehensive but it does aspire to be as comprehensive as possible. In particular, it misses out on many of the smaller academic journals. The core purpose of the ISI Web of Science has been to provide information on who is citing whom, to provide a faster way of finding articles which are related to each other and to provide an indication of how much impact individual journal articles have. It provides a way to trace long-term academic debates through the references writers make to those who have gone before them.

It has great strengths and significant weaknesses. All of the information is organized in rigidly codified databases, giving it a strong organizational structure. As a result, you don't pick up the irrelevant material and duplicate results that Google Scholar generates, and you can carry out very precise searches. On the other hand, the same rigidity means that your search options are sometimes restricted too tightly. You can't search for an author's full name, for example, only by their surname and initials, and the database can't distinguish between authors with the same surname and initials. If the author you're searching for has a common name, it can be difficult to get a full list of their publications. If you're searching for a publication title, you have to use the abbreviation ISI has assigned to it, leaving out common words like 'to' or 'the'. To do this often requires checking the 'cited work index' to see how ISI has abbreviated the publication. If the item you are looking for is a book, you may well find that it has been abbreviated in two or three different ways and that to pull together a full list of articles that cite it you will have to look at all of these entries. It is not at all uncommon for an article to be listed more than once with slightly different details. Thus it is very common for citations of a single article to be spread across two or more entries for the same article.

To bring back a list of articles that cite a particular article or book, do a 'Cited reference search' on the title and author. Click on the link to 'Times cited' to get a full list of all items which cite this article. You can then set up an alert to inform you when a new article also cites the same work. 'Find related records' brings back articles that cite any of the sources cited by the article you're looking at. This provides a powerful and novel way to identify clusters of related materials through shared references. ISI Web of Science also indexes book reviews, magazines and bibliographies, and allows you to restrict your search to a particular kind of item – to search only for bibliographies, for example. One major weakness of the service is the fact that it only deals with citations in articles and not in books.

Scopus

Established to rival ISI Web of Science as a major citation-based database, it is far easier to use. It is possible that your institution will only be subscribed to one or the other, given the expense involved. You can limit searches to social science materials but it is not particularly strong in this area, being stronger in the health and life sciences. It does not cover the humanities. The record for every article includes hyperlinks to articles that cite it and to articles that it cites. Unlike ISI Web of science, Scopus includes cited references from books. When you get a page of search results you can refine your search, limiting it to certain publications, authors and types of document. You can set up search alerts and citation alerts. It has far shallower historical coverage than ISI Web of science.

Other indexing and abstracting databases

PCI (Periodicals Contents Index) (**pcift.chadwyck.co.uk**)   PCI stands out for its historical depth, including items published two centuries ago and items in dozens of languages. It indexes around 15 million articles from over 4,000 journals in the humanities and social sciences. PCI also provides 'PCI Full Text', including the full text of a few hundred journals. It provides OpenURL links.

CSA Illumina (**www.csa.com**)   Illumina performs a joint search on over one hundred abstracting databases and full-text databases maintained by CSA, including specialized databases devoted to a variety of social science subjects. These subject databases are dealt with below on an individual basis. It provides OpenURL links.

Academic Search Premier (EBSCO)   Including academic journals, newspapers and magazines, it includes the full text of over 4,000 journals across a wide range of disciplines. It allows you to limit your search to academic journals and to limit it to full-text sources.

The International Bibliography of the Social Sciences   Focusing on anthropology, economics, politics and sociology, it indexes over 2,700 journals and around 7,000 books every year and is primarily aimed at UK universities. It has a strong focus on non-English language items that are neglected by many of the other databases. It indexes over 2 million items, including book reviews.

TABLE 3.1   Indexing and abstracting databases

Database	Subjects	Journals	Total records	Other materials	Additional features
OCLC ArticleFirst	Social sciences, humanities, popular culture	22,000+	19 million+	Current affairs magazines, reviews	Identifies libraries holding the journals
ISI Web of Science	Social sciences, humanities and science	1,730+		Reviews, magazines, bibliographies	'Cited reference search' and 'Find related records'
Scopus	All subjects	14,000+	27 million+	Conference proceedings, open access articles	Powerful reference linking
PCI	Humanities and social sciences	4,000+	15 million+		Deep historical coverage
CSA Illumina	All subjects				Joint search of over 100 CSA databases
Academic Search Premier	All subjects	4,000+ (full text)		Newspapers and magazines	
IBSS	Social sciences	2,700+	2 million+	Reviews 7,000+ books indexed every year	
Zetoc	All subjects	20,000+		16,000+ conference proceedings indexed per year	
Infotrieve	All subjects	54,000+	8.5 million+		

Ulrichsweb (**www.ulrichsweb.com**)   This directory of periodical publications and academic journals provides information on a far wider range of publications than any of the other databases listed here and is an excellent source of information on rare and obscure sources. It lists the abstracting and indexing services that each individual journal is included in. It also lists all of the full-text databases through which each journal can be accessed and provides OpenURL links to many of the articles listed.

Zetoc (**zetoc.mimas.ac.uk**)   This is the British Library's Electronic Table of Contents, a massive service indexing the contents of around 20,000 journals and 16,000 conference proceedings per year. It provides OpenURL links to the full text of articles, where available. It provides document delivery services to UK users. Like OCLC ArticleFirst, it indexes titles and keywords but not abstracts. British Library Direct (**direct.bl.uk**) is an electronic document delivery service that provides access for non-UK users to much of the material in the Zetoc database, a total of 9 million records from 20,000 journals.

Infotrieve ArticleFinder (**www.infotrieve.com**)   Infotrieve is primarily a document delivery service but you can also use it as a research resource. Select 'ArticleFinder' to search for academic articles. It searches abstracts and titles rather than full text. In the advanced search you can restrict your search by subject area, limiting it to the social sciences or humanities, for example.

   The total number of articles or journals does not provide the best indicator of a service's usefulness. A geography database with 100,000 records may well contain far more of use to a geographer than a database with 20 million records that covers everything from astrophysics to zoology. In Table 3.1 and the tables that follow, the figures given are minimum numbers. The numbers are constantly increasing. Different services estimate their total records and number of journals in very different ways and the figures listed here are not directly comparable. Nonetheless they do give a crude indication of the relative size of these databases.

 Search strategy: searching for an article

In the example below you have the details of an article you are interested in. Ideally, you want to get the full text but if you can't get that, you want to get enough information to tell you if it's worth ordering or purchasing. In the course of this search you also want to explore information associated with the article such as its references and the articles that cite it. For a research project on the academic debates around the

(Continued)

Harry Potter novels, for example, you might be interested in an article such as: Pennington, John (2002) 'From Elfland to Hogwarts, or the Aesthetic Trouble with Harry Potter', *The Lion and the Unicorn*, 26 (1): 78–97.

Google Scholar. Because Google Scholar (scholar.google.com) searches so many full-text databases simultaneously, you are highly likely to find the article in Google Scholar and it is the best place to start. If you don't find it in Google Scholar, the next step would be to search one of the large indexing and abstracting databases such as OCLC ArticleFirst, ISI Web of Science or Scopus.

The title of this article is so distinctive that a short snatch of the title, such as 'Elfland to Hogwarts', brings back the Google Scholar entry for the article. It also brings up two articles that cite it, both of them in the same journal, *The Lion and the Unicorn*:

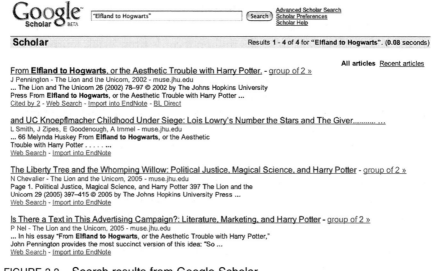

FIGURE 3.3   Search results from Google Scholar

The entry in Google Scholar for the article itself indicates that it's in a 'Group of 2', but when you click on this link you discover that these are duplicate results, both leading to the same site. The site is Project Muse, a full-text database that hosts *The Lion and the Unicorn*. If your library has a subscription to the journal you can get access to the full text at this point. If not, you are limited to viewing an excerpt from the text that gives a flavour of the contents.

The 'cited by' link in Google Scholar simply brings up the two articles already retrieved. The 'web search' link runs a query in ordinary Google on: "Pennington" "Elfland * Hogwarts or". This query is designed to ensure that it only returns pages that reference the article. This turns up links yet again to the Project Muse site but it also turns up a couple of useful course syllabi that reference the article. One of these courses devotes two classes to discussing a Harry Potter book and gives a few useful references that haven't turned up previously:

- Deconstructing Harry: Casting a Critical Eye on the Witches and Wizards of Hogwarts
- The Harry Potter Novels as a Test Case for Adolescent Literature

In the absence of a subscription to the journal, you can't get access via Google Scholar to the list of references cited by the article.

ISI Web of Science: In the 'General search' you can limit your search to the title of the article. In this example, the distinctive term 'Elfland' is enough to retrieve the short record for the article. If your library has enabled OpenURL linking, there will be an SFX or MetaLib or similar link here that will connect you to information about your library's holdings of online versions of this article. In my case, it shows that my library does not have the online version of the article.

The 'Times cited' link brings you to three articles that cite 'From Elfland to Hogwarts'. This includes two of the articles turned up by Google Scholar but it also turns up an additional article of interest:

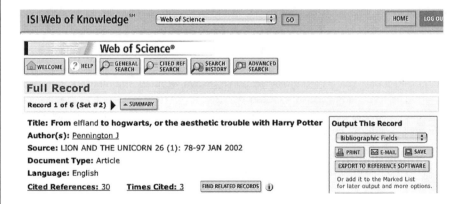

FIGURE 3.4   Extract from a record for an article in ISI Web of Science

- From world citizen to global player: 'Harry Potter' as cross-cultural phenomenon

In the short record for 'From Elfland to Hogwarts', click on the article title to get a fuller record. In the fuller record you can click on the author name to get a list of publications by the author. This example demonstrates the severe limitations of ISI Web of Science. The author's name is reasonably common and this brings back a list of 98 articles on a wide range of topics by several different authors with the same surname and first initial.

(Continued)

'Find related records' searches for other articles that share at least one reference with 'Elfland to Hogwarts' but in this case the search is of no value. It brings up 550 results, none of which shares more than two references with the article. Most of these refer to general texts on children's literature and there is nothing in the first page of results that seems to relate directly to Harry Potter.

The link to 'Cited references' provides an abbreviated list of the books and articles referenced in the article. The summary information provided is not enough to tell you much about these articles but it is enough to allow you to find them in ISI Web of Science if they look promising.

You can set up a citation alert for the article here, something that is not possible via Google Scholar. Every time a new article that cites 'Elfland to Hogwarts' is included in ISI Web of Science you will get an email letting you know.

OCLC ArticleFirst: In ArticleFirst the single word 'Elfland' in the title search box is enough to bring back the record for the article. The record provides information unavailable through any other source, providing a list of 646 libraries worldwide that stock the journal. Surprisingly, my library is among them, even though the OpenURL link in ISI Web of Science led nowhere. Although my library doesn't have access to the online version, the print version is sitting on the library shelves. The search for the full text is over. Clearly it was worth going beyond Google Scholar on this occasion. If the journal had not been available in my library, OCLC ArticleFirst would have shown me if it was available in a nearby library.

Ingenta: Oddly enough the word 'Elfland' does not retrieve the article in a title search of Ingenta (see below for more on Ingenta). The word 'Hogwarts' does retrieve it, indicating that these search technologies don't always work as smoothly as you might expect. The term 'Hogwarts' also retrieves 13 other articles, suggesting that it might be a useful search term to run on other article databases. Among the directly relevant articles it turns up are:

- Eichmann in Hogwarts: Harry Potter and the Banality of Evil
- Harry Potter and Philosophy: If Aristotle Ran Hogwarts
- What American Schools Can Learn from Hogwarts School of Witchcraft and Wizardry

Ingenta indexes *The Lion and the Unicorn* back to 1989 and you can click on the journal title to view tables of contents for every issue back to then, something it was not possible to do in ArticleFirst, ISI Web of Science or Google Scholar. You can quickly scan these contents pages to see if there are earlier relevant articles. You can also set up an alert to inform you when new issues of the journal are published.

Quick searches reveal that this journal is not available in SwetsWise, in Highwire, in CrossRef or in JSTOR.

Although there was a lot of overlap between the four services dealt with above, each of them provided significant information unavailable in any of the other services. In addition to this, several of the major services did not cover this journal at all.

Specialized subject databases

The central feature that marks these databases out from the big collections described above is exclusion. You can be sure that results will be tightly restricted to your subject area and closely related areas. If your research topic fits neatly within a single discipline, you may well find that it is much more fruitful to focus your searching on one of the databases below. You can do a quick mop-up search on the bigger databases later to make sure you haven't missed anything. Many of these specialized databases include abstracts written especially for these databases, covering not only articles but books too. In their concern to deal comprehensively with their particular subject area, they include relevant work from closely related disciplines and many of the smaller publications that are not indexed in any of the bigger databases. The list below includes many of the largest subject-specific abstracting and indexing databases in the social sciences and closely related disciplines in the humanities.

You can only get access to these databases if your institution is a subscriber, in which case there should be links from your institution's web pages. Several databases, including those hosted or run by CSA, now provide 'Cited Reference Linking' using OpenURL links to allow you to click directly from a cited reference to an abstract or the full text of the article cited, though this is generally only available for relatively recent articles. CSA also provide access to 'Scholar profiles' and 'Organization profiles', which provide information on researchers and research institutions.

Annual Bibliography of English Language and Literature (ABELL)   Articles, books and reviews on English language and literature from 1920 onwards, and in any language. Subjects covered include drama, poetry, fiction, biography, literary theory and film. It can also be accessed via *Literature Online* <**lion.chadwyck. co.uk**>

Anthropology Plus (includes archaeology)   Indexes articles, reports, commentaries and obituaries from nearly 900 journals and monographic series' from the nineteenth century onwards.

ASSIA: Applied Social Sciences Index and Abstracts (CSA)   Dealing with social science and health, it contains over 300,000 records from 650 journals.

CIOS ComAbstracts (**www.cios.org/www/abstract.htm**)   A database of article abstracts, books, bibliographic records and Internet materials on communication.

Columbia International Affairs Online (CIAO) (**www.ciaonet.org**)   A major international affairs database which includes academic working papers, occasional papers from non-governmental organizations (NGOs), research reports, policy briefs, conference proceedings, books, journals and case studies written specifically for inclusion in CIAO.

Communication Abstracts (CSA) Covers communications and closely related areas, including abstracts of articles, reports, papers and books.

FIAF: International Film Archive Indexes film and television periodicals, and film archives.

Geobase A database of journals, books, conference proceedings and reports, covering both physical and social geography. It provides abstracts for over 600,000 items. You can limit searches by subject category.

Historical Abstracts Abstracts of articles, books, dissertations and smaller publications not included in the bigger databases.

International Political Science Abstracts (IPSA) Produced by the International Political Science Association. Articles in languages other than English are abstracted in French. All titles are translated into English.

Linguistics & Language Behavior Abstracts (LLBA) (CSA) Books, journal articles and dissertations on linguistics and related disciplines.

Modern Language Association Bibliography (MLAIB) (CSA) Articles, books, dissertations, bibliographies, proceedings and other materials from the 1920s onwards on literature, language, cultural studies, linguistics, folklore, film and theatre. It includes materials in more than 60 languages.

PAIS International: Public Affairs Information Service (CSA) This service indexes over half a million journal articles, books, government documents, statistical directories, grey literature, research reports, conference reports, publications of international agencies, microfiche and Internet material. It has a strong international emphasis, including publications from over 120 countries and a large collection of materials in languages other than English.

Philosopher's Index (CSA) Articles, books, and book reviews on philosophy and closely related subjects, dating back to 1940.

Social Services Abstracts (CSA) Abstracts of journal articles from over 1,300 publications and abstracts of dissertations. It is focused on social work, human services and related areas, including social welfare, social policy and community development. It includes around 100,000 records.

Social Work Abstracts Produced by the US National Association of Social Workers, it includes over 45,000 records and dates back to 1977.

SocINDEX with Full Text (CSA) Abstracts for several hundred sociology journals and hundreds of related journals dating back to 1895. It also indexes books, conference papers, and a range of other sources. It contains full text for well over 300 journals, several hundred books and several thousand conference papers.

Worldwide Political Science Abstracts (CSA)   Citations and abstracts in political science and related areas, including international relations, law, and public policy. It includes around half a million entries and indexes about 1,500 journals and other publications, with a heavy emphasis on material published outside the USA.

TABLE 3.2   Subject databases

Database	Subjects	Journals	Records
ABELL	English language and literature		860,000+
Anthropology Plus	Anthropology and archaeology	*C.* 900	800,000+
ASSIA	Social science and health	500+	375,000+
CIOS	Communication		50,000+
CIAO	International affairs	*C.* 60	
Communication Abstracts	Communication	160+	49,000+
FIAF	Film	300+	325,000+
Geobase	Physical and social geography	2,000+	600,000+
Historical Abstracts	History	2,100+	600,000+
International Political Science Abstracts	Political Science	*C.*900	
Linguistics & Language Behavior Abstracts	Linguistics	1,500+	360,000+
MLAIB	Literature, language, cultural studies, film and theatre	4,400+	1.7 million+
PAIS International	International public affairs		550,000+
Philosopher's Index	Philosophy	550+	320,000+
Social Services Abstracts	Social work, social welfare, social policy, community development	1,300+	100,000+
Social Work Abstracts	Social work and closely related topics		45,000+
SocINDEX with Full Text	Sociology	Several hundred	1.6 million+
Worldwide Political Science Abstracts	Political science, international relations, public policy	1,500+	500,000+

Search strategy: searching by author

Locate a home page for an author by searching for author name and university on Google, Yahoo, MSNSearch or Ask.com. If somebody has written one good book or article in your area, chances are that they have written other material that might be useful to you. If an author does provide a home page it will often include some or all of the following:

- A fuller list of their publications than you'll get from any other source.
- Teaching syllabi and reading lists for their courses that may point you to other important sources in your area.
- Work in progress, which some authors make available online in order to advertise their work and to attract comments and suggestions.
- The full text of some of their articles.

Full-text articles online

Indexing and abstracting services can aspire to comprehensive coverage, or something close to it, because publishers are happy to have their articles indexed in all of these services, seeing it as a kind of advertising. Things are quite different when it comes to full text. Publishers make their money on selling the text. The full text is generally hosted by one service only, while the citation details and abstracts may be available in 20 different databases. As a result there is very limited overlap between full-text databases. The collections below each represent only a piece of the full-text puzzle. You can search many of these services via Google Scholar but it's always worth searching the full-text databases directly as well because they provide more powerful searching options.

SwetsWise (**www.swetswise.com**)   This is an aggregator service that allows libraries to manage their subscriptions to electronic journals. Unlike most of the services listed below, it does attempt to provide comprehensive coverage of full-text articles online from a variety of publishers. It doesn't host the content but it provides links to the full text of articles and information on whether your library subscribes or not. You can search titles, abstracts and keywords and limit your search by subject categories, but you can't search the full text of articles.

Highwire Press (**www.highwire.org**)   This is a non-profit full-text database that aims to make academic literature more widely available. A large proportion of the academic articles hosted here are available free of charge to anyone and Highwire is said to host the largest collection of free academic articles available. In addition, Highwire hosts the full-text collections of a number of major publishers, including Sage and Oxford University Press, adding up to a total of more than 800 journals. Like all full-text collections, it is far from comprehensive but as a collaborative project driven by academic as well as commercial concerns, it has very wide coverage.

One of the strongest features of Highwire is its links to other full-text services and to indexing and abstracting databases. You can link directly from Highwire to the full text of cited articles held in other databases (via CrossRef) and to information on articles that cite the article you're looking at in ISI's Web of Science, even if your institution does not subscribe to ISI Web of Science. It also provides links to the related entry in Google Scholar and to the citation search in Google.

You can limit your search to reviews and to specific subject categories. You can set up alerts to notify you when a particular article is cited, or when an item matching your search terms is added to the service. You can also sign up for contents alerting for journals included in Highwire, avoiding the need to sign up separately with several different publishers. An innovative feature called 'My Favorite Journals' allows you to limit your search to selected journals, allowing you to create a kind of personal search library.

Blackwell Synergy (**www.blackwell-synergy.com**)   A participant in CrossRef, Blackwell provides several advanced features that link it to the services of a range of other publishers and article databases. It includes over 600,000 articles from more than 800 journals, including most of the journals published by Blackwell.

Even if your library does not subscribe to a journal, you can view the abstracts of articles here, and follow links to 'citing articles' that cite the item you are looking at. You can view the list of references for an article. These references may include OpenURL links to your own library's holdings of the material in question. It also provides links to the records relating to these articles in a number of other databases that index and abstract them. Thus, it links to abstracts in ISI Web of science, to CSA Illumina (which includes the various CSA databases listed above) and directly to the full text article if it is held in Blackwell Synergy or a number of other full-text databases. You can sign up to receive an alert whenever a particular article is cited.

Ingenta Connect (**www.ingentaconnect.com**) Ingenta hosts full-text journals from a variety of academic publishers, attempting to offer a comprehensive collection of full-text articles online. It includes over 28,000 publications and 17 million articles and also searches abstracts of book chapters from Oxford Scholarship Online. You can search titles, abstracts and keywords but not the full text of articles. To search the full text you can use CrossRef or Google Scholar, although apparently they don't cover all of the articles held in Ingenta. You can only access the full text of an article if your library is a subscriber, but Ingenta offers a number of added features freely available to everyone, including links to 'Articles that cite this article'.

JSTOR (**www.jstor.org**) JSTOR is concerned to archive older issues of journals. As a result it has much greater historical depth than most full-text collections, going back to the late 1800s, when most full-text collections barely go back to the early 1990s. The collection includes important key journals in the social sciences and humanities under arrangements that specify a 'moving-wall' of three to five years. That is, publishers allow JSTOR to put articles online three to five years after they are published. You will often find that you have access to older articles in JSTOR from journals whose current contents you can't access. You can only get access if your library or institution has subscribed to JSTOR.

> **S**   Search strategy: keeping up with new articles

After you have mined the big databases you need an efficient way to keep up with the vast quantities of new material that are added regularly.

1. Content alerts

Set up content alerts for the three or four key journals in your area and perhaps a few others in related areas. Every time a new issue is published you will get an email listing the contents. You can set up these alerts through big databases such as Highwire Press, through the publishers (see below) or through the journal websites (search for the journal title in Google, Yahoo, Ask.com or MSNSearch).

2. Search alerts

In the course of your searching you will develop a few search queries that work particularly well. You can sign up in some services for search alerts that send you an email each time a new entry matching your search query is added.

3. Citation alerts

If you find citations of a key article or book produce a lot of useful leads, you can set up citation alerts to alert you when a new article cites this book or article. In many cases alerting results can now be imported directly into reference management software such as EndNote, Procite or Reference Manager.

Increasingly all of these alerting services are also available as RSS Feeds but email alerts are perfectly adequate.

Publishers

A single large publisher can be responsible for several hundred journals and several of the big publishers maintain control of the full text of their journals online, marketing and presenting them as discrete research collections. Some of these collections are massive and include many of the most prestigious journals, but they are still limited to the output of a single publisher. There are now multiple routes to the articles the publishers provide online. You can get to most of them from the big indexing services and to many of them from Google Scholar and via CrossRef, although you can always wring more out of the publisher sites by searching them individually.

You can search by author, title or abstract, search the full text of articles and download references in virtually all of the services listed below. Tables of contents and abstracts are usually freely accessible but access to the full text of journals is only available if your institution subscribes to the journal in question. The services below also offer a variety of advanced search options, including the option to restrict your search to certain subject areas or to limit it to your personal selection of journals. In some of the services you can limit your search to reviews or to certain types of article. Most of them also provide alerting services. Increasingly, these services provide extensive links to related materials. Oxford Journals, for example, provides links to 'Similar articles in ISI Web of Science' and links to citing articles in ISI Web of Science and Google Scholar.

* *Cambridge Journals Online* (**journals.cambridge.org**)
* *Elsevier Science Direct* (**www.sciencedirect.com**)
* *Oxford Journals Online* (**www.oxfordjournals.org**) Also available through Highwire Press
* *Project Muse* (**muse. jhu.edu**) Over 200 humanities and social sciences journals published by JHU Press and a number of other university presses
* *Sage Journals Online* (**Sagepub.com**) Also available through Highwire Press
* *SpringerLink* (**www.SpringerLink.com**)
* *Taylor and Francis Online Journals* (**www.tandf.co.uk/journals**)

TABLE 3.3   Full-text databases

Database	Coverage	Journals	Total records	Full-text search
Google Scholar	All subjects, wide range of academic publishers			Yes
CrossRef	All subjects, wide range of academic publishers		6.5 million+	Yes
SwetsWise	All subjects, wide range of academic publishers	17,000+	13 million+	No
Blackwell Synergy	Blackwell Journals	800+	600,000+	Yes
Ingenta Connect	All subjects, wide range of academic publishers	28,000+	17 million+	No
JSTOR	All subjects, wide range of academic publishers	580+	3 million+	Yes
Cambridge Journals Online	Cambridge Journals	180+		Yes
Elsevier Science Direct	Elsevier Journals	2,000+	6.7 million+	Yes
Highwire	All subjects, wide range of publishers	900+	3 million+	Yes
Oxford Journals Online	Oxford Journals (hosted by Highwire)	180+		Yes
Project Muse	Humanities and social sciences from several university presses	300+		Yes
Sage Journals Online	Sage Journals (hosted by Highwire)	320+	57,000+	Yes
SpringerLink	Springer Journals, and those of several other publishers	500+		Yes
Taylor and Francis	Taylor and Francis Journals	1,000+		Yes

Open access

The Internet is widely regarded as providing a unique historical opportunity for researchers to publish their own work online for little cost, bypassing the publishers. This dream of free circulation of academic work has not materialized. The publishers provide not only publication, but publicity, distribution and, above all, prestige, and it still makes sense for researchers to try to get published in the print journals. Nonetheless, there is an ongoing struggle to make academic work more widely available and increasing numbers of high-quality academic articles are now freely available online.

Contrary to expectations that the Internet would make academic journals cheaper, academic publishers are charging the same or even higher fees for access to journals online. In response to this, the open access movement has developed tools to allow academics to self-archive their published articles, either in 'institutional repositories' at their own universities or in subject-specific archives, making them freely available. Research funding agencies, governments and universities are beginning to wield their considerable financial power to pressurize academics to make their research more freely available through such repositories. In the face of evidence that open access articles are cited more frequently than those in pay databases (see Antelman, 2004, for example) even some publishers are beginning to think about moving in this direction. The open access movement is committed to high academic standards, with repositories generally limiting their collections to materials that have been through some kind of academic peer-review process.

The terms 'escholarship' and 'eprints' are used to refer to academic work made freely available online. 'Preprints' are earlier versions of articles, usually slightly different from the final published version, while 'postprints' are the final version, after all the recommended changes have been made. It is easier for academics to make preprints freely available and one difficulty with the repositories is that they are heavy with preprints, working papers, conference papers and other work that has not taken a final definitive form. You have to make it clear in your work that you are referring to such materials rather than to published articles. You may find that ultimately you need to get the final published version but at least the preprints allow you to decide how useful an article is to you. Open access repositories are searched by Google Scholar and are now included in several of the other indexing and full-text databases discussed above. This marks a recognition that they have become a major new source of academic literature beyond the published journals.

One of the main projects promoting the free circulation of academic publications is Highwire Press (www.highwire.org, see above). Although

Highwire Press also includes subscription journals, it makes it easier for open access journals to operate by providing an infrastructure for hosting the journals.

OAIster (**oaister.umdl.umich.edu/o/oaister**)   This search engine allows you to do a joint search of over 500 open access repositories. In early 2006 it included around 6 million records. It organizes the results by institution. It includes the full text of books in some cases and the full text of many PhD theses and dissertations. It also searches major academic resources on the open web through its inclusion of materials catalogued by services such as Humbul, the UK catalogue of online academic resources in the humanities.

FIGURE 3.5   OAIster

Directory of Open Access Journals (**www.doaj.org**)   A directory of around 2,000 free, full-text academic journals. You can do full-text searches of articles from around 500 of the journals.

Institutional repositories

Repositories differ in their criteria for inclusion. Some are more tightly restricted than others but materials have generally gone through an academic quality control procedure of some kind. Below are two well-known examples of open access repositories.

OU e-prints (**libeprints.open.ac.uk**)   The repository of the UK's Open University, it hosts research that has been authored or co-authored by members of staff. It only includes 'postprints', items which have been peer-reviewed or have gone through a similar process and which include the final changes made after review. It includes journal articles, book chapters and conference papers.

University of California eScholarship Repository (**repositories.cdlib.org/ escholarship**)   One of the earliest repositories, in 2006 it included over 10,000 items.

Other article databases

The databases dealt with below include collections of academic articles but they are dominated by news and current affairs sources. They are not targeted as directly at academic users as the services dealt with above. Once again, the amount of overlap between each of these services is huge, while they also overlap substantially with many of the academic databases.

LexisNexis (**www.lexisnexis.com**)   Before the public had ever heard of the Internet the business community was using powerful online databases such as LexisNexis that provided the full text of articles from a vast number of sources. These databases were so expensive and so complex to use that companies hired specialized searchers just to search them. The full text of articles is often available in LexisNexis within hours of their publication and the service allows very sophisticated searching. Articles are split into separate fields that can be searched separately. In recent years LexisNexis has expanded and developed services aimed at university students and researchers. The legacy of catering to highly trained and highly paid professional researchers is visible in the rather sparse instructions for use. LexisNexis is not concerned primarily with citation details but with providing fully searchable full-text articles. It covers thousands of newspapers and academic journals in addition to a wide range of specialized materials such as news broadcast transcripts that are extremely difficult to get hold of by any other means. It bundles its services to target academic users with packages such as LexisNexis Academic and LexisNexis Professional.

In LexisNexis Professional you can restrict searches to publications from particular countries, or to individual publications. A 'source directory' lists the different publications available to you. Including as it does vast numbers of newspaper stories, LexisNexis will generally return lots of results on all but the most specific queries. It is a good place to conduct very specialized searches using very specific phrases uniquely associated with your topic. Given the fact that the system balks if you return over 1,000 results, it's a good idea to limit your search by date, restricting it to a few years. Unlike many of the other commercial services that focus on newspaper and magazine articles, LexisNexis allows you to download references. Partly because they have been in the full-text business for so long, LexisNexis has the deepest historical coverage to be found anywhere of several major British and American newspapers.

Highbeam Research (**www.highbeam.com**)   Unlike most of the services dealt with above, Highbeam has flexible and reasonable pricing options aimed at users outside a university environment. It is far less powerful than the databases covered above, but can be useful if you don't have access to those, and also as part of a 'needle in the haystack' search to make sure you haven't missed anything. It seems to include a lot of very marginal and specialized publications and it is very strong on news and current affairs sources. The advanced search allows you to limit your search to certain kinds of material, to books, or newspapers or magazines for example, but not to academic articles, although Highbeam does include academic articles. It allows you to create a list of up to five selected publications and to limit your search to this selection. It also searches a variety of general encyclopaedias. They are not as specialized in the social sciences as those dealt with in Chapter 2, but if you are not affiliated to an institution they can be useful. You can choose 'reference' and then limit your search to encyclopaedias.

Find Articles (**www.findarticles.com**)   Including over 10 million articles, Find Articles is dominated by material from magazines and newspapers but also includes a large number of academic journals. A lot of these articles are actually hosted on Highbeam, however, and there appears to be a large overlap in content between the two services. Many of the articles are available for free and you can limit your search to free articles. You cannot download references and search options are not very sophisticated.

Theses and dissertations

Many high-quality theses and dissertations are never published despite the fact that they contain valuable material of use to other researchers. There are a few online services now devoted to providing not only bibliographic detail about theses and dissertations, but to making the full text available, sometimes for a fee. In addition, the full text of many theses and dissertations is now freely available through open access repositories, which are searchable through *OAIster* (**oaister.umdl.umich.edu/o/oaister**), discussed above. If you are doing an extensive piece of research, it is almost certain that there will be a few theses or dissertations of use to you, which contain valuable material not available elsewhere.

ProQuest Dissertations & Theses (**wwwlib.umi.com/dissertations**)   A searchable database of abstracts, keywords chosen by the authors and basic citation information like title, date of submission and author. Coverage is not very deep in historical terms, going only as far back as the 1980s and 1990s in the case of many universities covered. Theses and dissertations completed since 1997 are available as PDF files, with a preview of the first 20 or so pages freely available to users at institutions that are subscribed. The full text of these theses and dissertations is instantly downloadable for a fee. The database is limited to items from universities that have arrangements with the database company. While virtually all North American universities are included, coverage is much patchier elsewhere in the world and is far from comprehensive.

Index to Theses (**www.theses.com**)   A database of abstracts and citation details of masters and doctoral theses accepted by universities in Great Britain and Ireland. It covers the period from 1970 onwards. Thus it has deeper historical coverage than dissertation abstracts while covering only the UK and Ireland. As a result it contains much material not found in any other database. Once again it is not to be regarded as comprehensive, even within the limited realm which is its concern. You can only get access if your library subscribes to the service. You can order copies of British theses through the *British Thesis Service* (**www.bl.uk/britishthesis**) of the British Library.

Networked Digital Library of Theses and Dissertations (**vtls.com/ndltd**)   This service draws on collections of 'Electronic Theses and Dissertations' archived online at a number of universities and a few larger commercial services. It provides the full text of dissertations, downloadable as PDF documents, often free of charge. Quite a limited number of theses and dissertations are available.

Dissertation.com (**www.dissertation.com**)   This commercial service provides the full text of dissertations via the Internet, for a fee. It also allows you to order theses and dissertations as bound copies via Amazon.com. You can search for dissertations by keyword or browse through lists of dissertations grouped by subject. There is a very limited selection.

Exercises

Exercise1: Finding an article

Identify a key article on your topic. Search for the article using all of the following services that you have access to:

- OCLC ArticleFirst
- ISI wORLDWeb of Science and/or Scopus
- Swetsnet

(Continued)

- Google Scholar
- Highwire Press
- Ingenta
- The journal publisher's full-text service (where one exists)
- A specialized subject database
- LexisNexis

In the case of each service answer the following questions:

- Does it include the article you're searching for?

If it does:

- Does it provide a link to the full text?
- What other links does it provide in relation to the article?
- How useful are these links?
- What additional information does it provide about the article?
- Can you download references?
- What is the best feature of this service?
- What are the weaknesses of this service?

Describe the extent of the overlap between the various services.

If you could only use one source, which would you use? Why?

Exercise 2: Searching by author

Locate a home page for the author of a useful article or book on your topic by searching for author name and university on Google, Yahoo, Ask.com or MSNSearch. Add the title of one of the author's publications to the search terms if necessary. Try to choose an author with several publications in your area. Note that many authors will not make any information available online. If you can't find a home page for one author, just keep trying different authors until you find a home page.

Look on the author's home page for lists of the author's publications, teaching syllabi, reading lists and the full text of their publications, where available. If the home page contains little information, search their university's site to see if information on the author's courses or their research record is available elsewhere on the site.

- Describe any difficulties you had in finding an author's home page.
- Describe the information you found.

For the same author, search for all articles by the author in:

- OCLC First Search
- ISI Web of Science and/or Scopus
- Google Scholar

Compare and contrast the search results from these three services with each other and with the results from the author's home page.

- How much overlap is there?
- Which of these sources provided the most comprehensive results?

Exercise 3: Setting up alerts

Identify two key journals in your area. Set up content alerts for these journals. Briefly describe any difficulties in setting up the alerts.

Set up a search alert for a specialized search query that has already returned useful results for you from the article databases. Briefly describe any difficulties in setting up the alert.

Set up a citation alert for a key article or book in your area. Briefly describe any difficulties in setting up the alert.

Exercise 4: Searching by citation

Select one key article and one key book relevant to your research. The aim of your search is to find books and articles that cite them, on the assumption that some of them will be directly relevant to your research. If your selected book or article does not turn up any references, try another book or article.

1. Search Google Scholar using the title and author name

- Follow the 'cited by' links for all versions of the article or book returned in the results page.
- List all of the unique sources that cite your book or article.
- How many of the sources that cite your article or book are themselves academic books and articles?
- How much duplication is there in the Google results?

2. Search ISI World of Science (a 'cited reference search') or Scopus using the title and author surname

In ISI World of Science you will often need to abbreviate titles, leaving out common words such as the, to, from, and. If you can't guess the abbreviation, you'll have to go to the 'cited work index' to see how they have abbreviated the item you're looking for.

(Continued)

- List all of the unique sources that cite your book or article. Select one that seems relevant to your research and then click on 'find related records'. List the first ten sources that this turns up. How relevant are these results?
- Which of the two services was more difficult to use? Why?
- Which of the services turned up the most useful sources?
- How much overlap is there between the sources they turned up?
- What are the drawbacks of each of these services?
- If you had to choose just one service to do a citation search on, which would you choose and why?
- Is it worth searching both of the services you searched or is the overlap too large to make it worthwhile?

Exercise 5: Searching for a needle in a haystack

Choose a phrase uniquely associated with a specialized aspect of your topic. Search for the exact phrase in the following services. If the phrase is bringing back too many irrelevant results, choose a different phrase or refine the search by adding another term uniquely associated with your topic. If it brings back no results, choose another term.

Search at least five of the services listed below:

- Amazon.com
- Amazon.co.uk
- Google Book Search
- Google Scholar
- Ingenta
- Highbeam
- LexisNexis

In relation to each service you use:

- List the useful results.
- Discuss the extent of the overlap between the results retrieved by the different services.

4
Subject guides

Searching the open Web

The previous two chapters on books and articles focused on highly structured databases. This chapter and chapters deal with the open web, online
resources that lie beyond those databases.

Whatever subject area you are interested in there is a strong chance that
someone has produced a guide to online resources on the topic. A good
guide provides one of the best ways to identify the central online resources
in your area. When you start devising queries for the big keyword search
engines you can concentrate on mopping up things that were missed by the
guides. These guides vary in quality. The best of them amount to advanced
annotated bibliographies, introducing you to resources in a very specific
area. The worst of them are so broad and unfocused as to be useless. These
guides are also referred to as indexes, catalogues, directories, gateways and
clearing houses.

Making sense of the chaos

Before exploring the guides it is useful to understand how things are organized on the open web. There is a deep-seated reason for the disorganiza-
tion on the open web. There is a lack of agreed universal standards for the
core elements that a web document should include. Email messages
may seem as difficult to order and categorize as web pages but in email the
software forces the key identifying marks of sender, recipient address and
date on to every email. All of these can be used to set items in their proper
context, as part of a particular discussion at a particular time. Web documents, by contrast, share only one universal identifying mark, their URL,
the Uniform Resource Locator, which usually starts with **http://** and
which is also referred to as the web address or the Internet address. Even
this can shift and change. If the person in charge of a particular web

document decides to rename the document or to move it around on his or her own computer, the URL changes. To compound the problem, the contents of web documents change, unlike printed matter and email messages. The same document at the same URL with the same title and author can have very different contents depending on when you look at it.

Sometimes it can take some serious detective work to even identify the author of a document. Finding out when it was written is often impossible and identifying the wider site or collection it is part of can require a fairly advanced understanding of the different ways in which websites are organized. Even major organizations often neglect to clearly stamp their authority on the documents they put on the web. You will often read about the lack of central authority and control on the Net but it is this lack of agreed standards at a fundamental level which is perhaps the most deeply rooted source of the chaos. Having said all this, the bulk of well-established organizational websites, be they universities, governments, political parties, businesses or others, organize their sites clearly and coherently. The web may be a swirling mess and you may reach such sites by a circuitous route, but once you are there you will generally find that documents are well organized, and will all have key identifying marks like author and date. While such sites are well structured, they are often structured very differently from one another.

Memory, forgetting and the Internet Archive

Huge volumes of material disappear from the Internet every day as the people running websites update their materials or allow their sites to become defunct. A webmaster who drags a document from his or her website to the trash may well be destroying the only copy of that information in existence anywhere. Even if a webmaster wants to preserve older versions of documents, there are no well established and widely used standards for archiving out-of-date web documents. As a consequence, those archives of web documents that do exist vary greatly in their organization and structure. The result of this lack of concern for memory and archiving is that a huge volume of information is wiped off the Net every day and disappears entirely from the historical record. Materials that were online only a few years ago might as well never have existed. One major project, *The Internet Archive* (**www.archive.org**), is attempting to ensure that these materials are saved, but they are limited in the volume of information they can save. Very often they archive only a few sample pages from a site and they often miss out on images and other features of websites that are difficult to archive.

When the Internet Archive was first established it seemed an eccentric kind of venture. Few people saw the point of saving copies of websites that everyone already had access to. Just a few years on we are already beginning to appreciate just how important it is. Millions of sites have vanished over the past few years and millions of others have changed beyond recognition. The Internet Archive provides the only means of knowing that most of these sites ever existed. The Archive saves websites at regular intervals, every few weeks or months. When you go to the Archive you can explore how a website looked at various intervals during its history. If you are carrying out research on an organization of any kind, you may well find yourself using the Internet Archive to track the changes in the way that organization has represented itself online. These changes can be very revealing. Organizations often remove materials because they change their policies or because they realize that the materials show them in a bad light. To see the archives for an individual website or web page, type the URL into the Internet Archive's *Wayback Machine*.

The Archive has worked in partnership to develop a number of specialized collections. One of the best known of these is the *September 11 Web Archive* (**lcweb4.loc.gov/911/**), a collection of more than 30,000 websites about the September 11 attacks that appeared in the three months after the attacks.

The Archive faces one major difficulty. The owners of domain names can block the Archive from making materials from that domain available to the public. This fact has punched huge holes in the Archive and means that organizations have the right to cover their tracks, to effectively destroy the previous records of materials they made available publicly. It also means that someone can buy the domain name of a defunct organization and then block public access to the archives of an organization they might have nothing to do with.

FIGURE 4.1   The Internet Archive

Academic subject guides

The services dealt with here follow academic classification schemes and cater specifically to academic researchers. They organize material according to disciplines and specialist areas within those disciplines. They provide an excellent starting point for an initial exploration of online resources in your subject area.

Intute (www.intute.ac.uk)

Intute is a collection of subject directories that serve the academic community in the UK but are freely available to everyone. In gathering together links to the relevant journals, professional associations, data sources and article collections in each subject area, these directories do much more than provide a set of hyperlinks. They provide an introduction to the subject areas and sub-disciplines they cover.

Intute: Social Sciences   The heart of the Intute social sciences directory is a service that used to be known as SOSIG (Social Sciences Information Gateway). It concentrates on identifying key resources in major areas rather than producing guides to very specialized topics. However, every sub-section also provides a list of 'Resource Guides', pointing you to other online guides in that subject area that are generally far more specialized. Thus, it is not only an important subject guide in its own right, but also one of the best ways to identify other subject guides in your field.

In every subject section, online resources are grouped according to the same set of categories. Among the most useful of these categories is the 'Editor's Choice', which identifies a small set of key resources. Other categories include 'Research Projects/Centres', linking you to academic research units specializing in the relevant area, and 'Papers/Reports/Articles (collections)', which links you to major collections of full-text articles in the area.

The 'Mailing Lists/Discussion Groups' category provides one of the best ways to identify useful mailing lists in your area from among the thousands of lists available, while 'Bibliographic Databases' points you to specialized subject databases that are often unknown to anyone outside the field.

The directory tries to be comprehensive and every subject category and sub-category has plenty of items in it. Each record contains a description of the resource linked to and a set of keywords for that resource. Many of the subject sections are maintained by academic institutions or organizations which have an expertise in the subject area. You can restrict a keyword search to a particular subject category by choosing 'current section' from within the category. More recently, certain sections of the directory have begun to cooperate more closely with subject directories that belong to the World Wide Web Virtual Library (see below). This promising development should strengthen both services.

Intute: Arts and Humanities   This directory is based to a large extent on the subject gateway previously known as Humbul Humanities Hub. Each entry is tagged with a number of subject headings and can be found listed under any of those headings. You can also search by resource type within any subject area, allowing you to identify key resource guides, mailing lists, databases and other resources in your subject area. Searching 'By Intended Audience' is an unusual but useful feature that allows you to separate resources intended for academic faculty and postgraduates from those aimed at undergraduates.

Other guides to academic resources

The Virtual Library (**www.vlib.org**)   The World Wide Web Virtual Library is the original guide to academic subject guides, established in 1991. The Virtual Library appears to the user as a single organization, providing hundreds of guides on a vast array of subjects. It is effectively an umbrella title covering guides which vary widely in quality and which are nearly all produced by different individuals and organizations. Some of the Virtual Library guides are huge complex services in their own right, such as the Virtual Library on Migration and Ethnic Relations (**www.ercomer.org/wwwvl**) run by ERCOMER (European Research Center on Migration and Ethnic Relations). The areas covered by the guides are determined by those who create them, and as a result coverage is very uneven. Those who produce the guides have to sign up to certain minimal common standards.

BUBL Information Service (**www.bubl.ac.uk**)   Primarily aimed at the UK academic community, this service, based at the University of Strathclyde, classifies resources according to the Dewey subject classification system used in many libraries. You can search by subject category and classification number. It focuses on major resources and provides short and precise descriptions of sites.

Infomine (**infomine.ucr.edu**)   Infomine is the Scholarly Internet Resource Collections produced by librarians from several campuses in the University of California system. It is extremely well organized. Entries are classified by subject area and are given associated keywords. It is organized by subject, including a category for 'Social Sciences and Humanities'. You can browse the subject categories and you can also search by keyword. It provides short descriptions of the sites it links to.

Librarians' Internet Index (**lii.org**)   A guide to Internet resources that have been evaluated by librarians. It has a heavy emphasis on academic sources and includes 'Arts and Humanities' and 'Social Science' sections. The Index focuses on key sites and provides useful short descriptions of every site included.

Internet Public Library (**www.ipl.org**)   A guide to Internet resources organized by subject category. A keyword search brings up related categories as well as individual records.

Professional Associations   Academic professional associations sometimes provide guides to online resources in their subject area. Many of these associations also have specialist groups and some of these also provide guides to online resources in their area of specialization. You can identify the relevant associations through the links in the Intute directories (**www.intute.ac.uk**) or through the guide to professional associations provided by the *Scholarly Societies Project* (**www.scholarly-societies.org**).

H-Net (**www.h-net.org**)   The H-Net discussion lists cover a range of areas in the social sciences and the humanities. All of the lists have websites and many of them provide guides to online resources in their area. These guides are particularly valuable because of the subject expertise involved, the focus on academic resources and the focus on major key resources.

Wikipedia (**www.wikipedia.org**)   Wikipedia entries generally include a list of recommended websites. In many cases these are either guides to online resources on the topic in question or key sites on the topic. You have to remain aware, however, that there isn't the same level of quality control as there is in the organized academic guides described above.

 Search strategy: exploring academic subject guides

Exploring a few major guides to online resources in your research area provides a way to quickly identify key online resources. For a research project on the politics of international football you might begin by looking for a guide to online resources on the sociology of sport, a broad area that covers your topic. Because this is such a clearly demarcated, and popular, subject area, it is easy to find a guide by checking the sociology section of the *Intute: Social Sciences* guide. One of the 24 sociology sub-sections here is devoted to the sociology of sport. It identifies several key journals in this area, and an email list on the topic.

The organizations/societies heading includes a link to the *International Sociology of Sport Association*. Professional associations like this generally provide guides to resources in their area and the ISSA guide turns out to be a focused collection of online resources on the sociology of sport. It includes links to sociology of sport journals not included in the Intute guide as well as links to the *North American Society for the Sociology of Sport*, to research centres on 'sport and society' and to a 'Scholarly Sport site' that acts as a guide to academic resources on sport in general. The *North American Society* site in turn includes a blog that is used to distribute information on jobs, conferences, and scholarships related to the sociology of sport and provides its own guide to online resources.

All of these guides provide links to research centres such as the *Centre for the Sociology of Sport* at the University of Leicester in the UK. Research centres often provide guides of their own to online resources in the area. In addition, some of them provide archives of publications by members of staff and an eclectic set of materials on the subject that can be of use to a researcher.

Most of these guides also provide a link to the 'Virtual Laboratory for Leisure, Tourism & Sport', a set of 70 specialized bibliographies including a 'sport and politics' bibliography that provides a list of more than 100 journal articles, several of which are directly relevant to the politics of international football.

You can continue to search for related resources in the other academic subject guides, but this quick sweep through guides identified via Intute has already turned up a number of key resources that are listed in several different guides.

Flexibility is important in this search. It is not a matter of exhaustively exploring every resource listed in every guide, but of hopping from guide to guide, identifying two or three new resources in each guide, and using the guides themselves to identify other guides. It doesn't especially matter where your search begins or ends. There is a huge amount of overlap between all of these guides and you will quickly reach the point of diminishing returns.

The result of this exploration is a list of around ten major online academic resources, ranging from a specialist bibliography through mailing lists and blogs to journals, professional associations and key research centres. When you begin to do keyword searches of the open Web through the big search engines you will find that many of the hits you bring back will come from these key sites. Quickly getting to know the key resources in your area will make subsequent keyword searching much easier and faster.

If your subject area is as clearly titled and demarcated as 'sociology of sport' is, a simple keyword search on one of the big search engines can often provide a perfectly good starting point for exploring guides on the topic. A Google search on **"sociology of sport"**, for example, brings back tens of thousands of hits but among the first ten results are several of the key resources in the area, including the Intute section on 'sociology of sport'. Because the search term is used in the title of subject guides, research centres, journals and professional associations, these large and popular sites come to the top of the search results.

Universal subject guides

The Internet is full of subject directories that partition the entire world of human knowledge into browseable subject headings. Their ambitions are universal, aiming to guide you to everything from cars and holidays to zoology and astrophysics. Because they cover a lot, it's difficult for them to cover any one thing particularly well. The best of these guides come into their own in providing lists of things which fall naturally into list form, like sports teams, newspapers, universities or towns – anything that can be easily classified and categorized.

The main problem with these guides is that they exercise minimal quality control and include links of very poor quality, barely relevant to the category they've been included in. They often miss the central resources on a particular subject because they make no attempt to be comprehensive. They generally provide no description or minimal description of the resources they link to and they don't emphasize academic resources. Having said all this, it is well worth while to quickly trawl the two major directories listed below to find sub-sections related to the topic you're interested in, but only after you have used the academic guides listed above. Unlike the academic guides, they often have sections on very specialized and obscure topics if those topics also happen to be of great public concern and interest.

Yahoo! Directory (**dir.yahoo.com**)   When you search the Yahoo Directory, the results at the top of the page are Yahoo subject categories that include your search term. These are followed by individual web pages that are catalogued in the Directory. Only a tiny proportion of web pages have been included in the Directory but it is still vast. Every category within Yahoo has its own web page. Each of these pages contains links to external web pages which fit into that category, and links to Yahoo sub-categories within that category. Only at the very bottom of the Yahoo subject tree will you find pages that only have external links. At the higher levels category pages consist primarily of links to sub-categories. Social science is one of the main top-level categories in Yahoo. It has over 40 sub-categories. The numbers after the name of a category indicates how many links are included in that category. This includes the total number of all links within the sub-categories that come under that category. The higher-level categories are not necessarily the best sources of good links. Cataloguers put resources in the lowest-level category they can.

Many sub-categories fit into several different higher-level categories. The way Yahoo deals with this is to try to include sub-categories in all of the higher-level categories they belong to. Thus the Yahoo 'Peace and Conflict Studies' page includes a link to the sub-category 'Regional conflicts'. There is an @ sign after the name of the sub-category. This indicates that it is listed here for convenience but that it is actually located on another branch of the Yahoo subject tree, in this case the 'Politics' branch. External links are frequently listed in two different categories. As a result, certain categories in entirely different branches of the subject tree are almost identical in their contents.

YAHOO! SEARCH Directory

Search: ⦿ the Web | ◯ the Directory | ◯ this category

Social Science > Peace and Conflict Studies   Email th

Directory > Social Science > **Peace and Conflict Studies**

CATEGORIES (What's This?)

- **Conferences** (4)
- **Conflict Resolution** (43)
- **Education** (21)
- **Human Rights@**
- **Institutes** (16)
- **Journals** (6)
- **Migration and Ethnic Relations@**
- **Organizations** (16)
- **Peace and Nonviolence@**
- **Regional Conflicts@**
- **War Reporting@**

FIGURE 4.2   Yahoo 'Peace and Conflict Studies' category

Yahoo provides several national versions of its service. Yahoo UK and Ireland (**uk.yahoo.com**) and Yahoo Germany (**de.yahoo.com**) were among the first. The subject categories are generally the same as in the main Yahoo version but with additional categories and sub-categories of special relevance to the country concerned and additional links to sites relevant to the country. You have the option to limit your search to sites related to the country involved. If you are searching for material in a language other than English, you should certainly search the Yahoo for the country where that language is the main language. Sites in languages other than English are generally not included in the main Yahoo Directory if there is a national Yahoo where that language is the main language.

The Open Directory Project (**dmoz.org**)   The Open Directory looks very similar to Yahoo but there is a radical difference. Volunteers maintain the directory categories. This creates problems but it also means that many of the Open Directory categories are maintained by enthusiastic experts who know quite a bit about their area. The contents of the categories and even the categories themselves are very different from those in the Yahoo Directory. The Open Directory uses the same kind of subject tree structure as Yahoo and its layout is very similar. When you search Google Directory (**directory.google.com**) you search the contents of the Open Directory. If you choose to search it via Google, you will get a lot more results and a more sophisticated search, but this can sometimes make it more difficult to identify the relevant categories.

S Search strategy: exploring the universal subject guides

The universal subject guides don't generally include specialized academic guides but they provide many excellent guides to issues of current controversy and debate.

The construction by Israel of a 'Separation barrier' in the Palestinian territories under Israeli occupation is exactly the kind of current issue that the universal guides deal with well. There are two general approaches to identifying a guide to online resources on this issue. The first is to do a broad keyword search to identify the relevant categories in the guides that might include material on this topic. The second is to search on a term uniquely associated with your subject to pull up very specific web pages catalogued in the directory. These then point you to the relevant category they have been classified under.

A search in the Open Directory (**dmoz.org**) on **Israel** brings up five categories with Israel in the title. One of these is a guide to online resources on conflict in Israel/Palestine. This guide provides a long list of other guides on the conflict that can be explored in turn. It also includes a section on the 'occupation' that includes one item dealing directly with the barrier. A search on the more specific term **"Separation Barrier"** turns up no results.

A search in the Yahoo Directory on **Israel** brings up several categories but none of them seems directly relevant. A search on **"separation barrier"** on the other hand, brings up two results that both belong to a Yahoo category entirely devoted to the 'Israeli West Bank Barrier'. This category points to ten major resources on the topic and provides a very useful starting point for exploration.

Wikipedia has good academic coverage in many areas but it can also be an excellent source of guides to topics of public debate. A search in Wikipedia on **"separation barrier"** brings up an entry which points to the Wikipedia entry on 'Israeli West Bank barrier'. This is a long article summarizing the political debates around the issue. At the end of the article there is a well-organized list of online resources on the topic, which acts as an excellent and extensive guide. It is significantly more useful than either the Yahoo or Open Directory guides on the same topic and includes virtually all of the resources identified by both of these, along with several others.

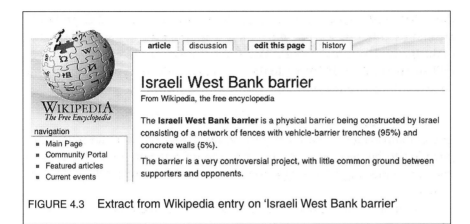

FIGURE 4.3   Extract from Wikipedia entry on 'Israeli West Bank barrier'

About.com   This provides a collection of several hundred subject guides, organized by subject category. A large number of the guides relate to areas of current political controversy, and these are to be found under the 'News and Issues' subject heading. Each of the guides is run by an individual who often puts a personal stamp on the guide. About.com has direct authority over the guides it provides, commissioning guides on particular subjects, trying to ensure the guides have the same basic format and are all part of a single, coherent service. As a commercial company whose priorities are not shaped by academic research interests, it has few guides to obscure areas of academic interest. The guides are rich in description of the sites they link to but they vary widely in quality.

Understanding web addresses

The URL or web address can quickly reveal information about a document that it would take much longer to find out by other means and can help you to assess documents quickly. They are essential to understanding how websites are organized.

Protocol
The first part of any web address is the protocol. The protocol used for web pages is the HyperText Transfer Protocol (http) so web addresses generally begin with **http://**. The :// separates the protocol from the rest of the address. Some URLs begin with **https://**. This indicates that there is an extra level of encryption at this site to facilitate secure and confidential communication, such as credit card transactions.

Among the other major protocols you will encounter are **rss://, gopher://, telnet://** and **ftp://**. RSS, indicating a link to a news feed, is the only one of these that most Internet users will regularly encounter. The other protocols are still used but they were much more important during an earlier stage of the Internet, before the World Wide Web existed. The main web browsers will automatically add **http://** to the start of any address you type in if you have not done so already.

Domain name

The domain name is the main part of any URL. The domain names are intended to be descriptive and to provide information about the service you are connecting to. A single computer may host thousands of domain names.

The domain name shown in Figure 4.4 illustrates the way in which these addresses are composed. The last part of the domain name is the top-level domain – .edu in the example in Figure 4.4 – indicating that this is a US university. The middle part, anycollege, is the name of the imaginary university. The first part, **www**, is the server name or host name. It could just as easily be called 'Fred' or 'Matilda', and some of them are. Note that while the domain name is not case sensitive, the file path that follows it is.

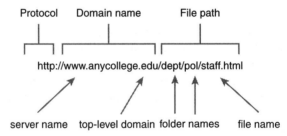

FIGURE 4.4   The structure of a web address

 Technical information: IP addresses

Every computer connected directly to the Internet (that is, not through another computer via a modem) has a unique IP address consisting of four sets of numbers, such as 127.131.10.176. The computer's domain name is just an alias for this number. In routing messages and requests across the Internet, it is these numbers that are used. They are the 'real' address.

When you make a request for a web page at a certain domain the first thing your computer has to do is look up the 'real' address for this domain name. It checks the nearest DNS server (Domain Name System), which keeps tables of the IP addresses.

Top-level domains

The last part of a domain name is the top-level domain. It tells you what country the computer is registered in or, in many cases, what type of organization runs the computer. 'Country code' top-level domains are often easy to guess, like **.ca** for Canada, **.jp** for Japan, **.ru** for Russia. There is a top-level domain for every country in the world and a list is available online (**www.iana.org/cctld/cctld-whois.htm**). They always consist of two letters. 'Generic' top-level domains, by contrast, have three letters and tell you what type of organization runs the web server you have connected to. They reflect the US origins of the Internet. The US government, US universities and the US military were heavily involved in the development of the Net at the initial stages. As a result, they each got their own top-level domain.

Thus **.mil** is the top-level domain for the US military and the US military alone. **.edu** is short for educational institution, but the only educational institutions that use this top-level domain are US universities. **.gov** stands for government, the US government. Things are a little less clear-cut in the case of the other category domains. **.com** stands for commercial sites and while a huge proportion of **.com** domains are US-based, anyone, anywhere in the world can easily get a **.com** address. **.org** was intended to be the domain for non-commercial organizations but is now open to everyone. It includes political parties in countries outside the USA as well as international organizations and non-governmental organizations (NGOs). **.int** is theoretically for international organizations but some of the largest of these are in the **.org** domain, including the United Nations and the OSCE (Organization for Security and Cooperation in Europe). NATO, on the other hand, uses the **.int** domain. **.net** was intended for organizations concerned with the administration and development of the Internet, but anyone can now get a **.net** address. A brief explanation of the generic domains is provided online by the *Internet Assigned Numbers Authority* (**www.iana. org/gtld/gtld.htm**).

Virtually all Internet Service Providers (ISPs) and all free web space providers use the **.com** domain. Lots of small organizations use web space provided by one or other of these sources and therefore the web addresses end in .com. Just because their web addresses include **.com** does not mean that they are commercial sites. **.us** is the country domain for the USA, but the vast majority of US sites do not use this domain.

People all over the world can register in the domains **.int, .org**, and **.com**, but a large proportion of those outside the USA register in their country domains. The country domains are complicated as well. Just because a computer is registered in a certain country does not mean it is located in that country. Certain poorer countries that have domain names that are commercially attractive have taken to selling names to the highest bidder, no matter where they are based. There is no guarantee that a domain ending in **.tm** is actually located in Turkmenistan, for example. The central

Asian republic has been selling domain names to US companies who treat the **.tm** as short for trademark. Likewise, the tiny pacific island of Tonga is not actually home to the many websites which have registered there simply for the purpose of having a domain name ending in **.to,** such as **come.to**, **welcome.to** and so on.

Several countries outside the USA have set up organizational domains of their own within the country domain. Thus the UK has **ac.uk** (academic community, i.e., universities), **co.uk** (commercial companies) and **gov.uk** (the UK government). In Australia **edu.au** is for universities, **org.au** for organizations. Japan has **go.jp** for government sites and **ac.jp** for universities.

 Technical information: port numbers

Sometimes you will come across a domain name that includes an odd-looking number, like **www.anycollege.edu:80.** This is a port number. A web server can allow access through several different ports. When you connect to the domain name on its own with no number, you connect through the default port (usually port 80). Some webmasters used to add the port number to their web address to make doubly sure people could connect, but this is no longer very common.

The path

After the domain name comes the path, **/depts/pol/staff.html** in the example in Figure 4.4 above. The path, as its name suggests, lays out a path to the particular file you want. Each forward slash separates one folder from another until the last item, which is the name of the file you want to retrieve, in this case, **staff.html.**

When you connect to the address in the example in Figure 4.4, your computer essentially asks the web server, 'please open the folder **depts**, then open the folder **pol** which is inside it. In that is a file called **staff.html.** Please send it to me.' You can often tell quite a lot from the path. Here, for example, it seems likely that **staff.html** is a list of staff in the politics department.

Understanding websites

The website a document belongs to provides the context within which that document can be understood, situating it as part of a collection of related documents. To use a web page without knowing what site it belongs to can be a bit like using a photocopied page without knowing anything about the book it is copied from. Understanding how websites are organized is essential to understanding the context of the materials that you find online. It will also help you to make much more efficient use of both the subject guides and the keyword search engines.

Defining site

'Website' is not as simple a concept as 'book'. A website may well be the online equivalent of a book, with the various chapters organized as separate web pages. It might equally be the equivalent of a magazine, a journal, an archive or a collection of any of these. A site may take full advantage of the potential of hypertext and be organized in a way for which there is not even a remote equivalent in print. A broad definition of 'website' might describe it as consisting of all of the materials placed together on the Web by a particular organization or project or individual. The central question is 'whose' site you are looking at. Sites, thus defined, can be massive. The Boston College site (**www.bc.edu**), the Irish government site (**www. irlgov.ie**), the US House of Representatives site (**www.house.gov**), all contain numerous sub-sections. It can also mean a tiny collection of documents put on the Web by a single individual or even a single document if it is genuinely not part of any larger organizing structure. The key element is authority.

Most large organizational sites consist of thousands of documents organized in many different sub-sections. It is often necessary to identify the particular sub-section of a site a document belongs to in order to understand it fully. Thus, to understand a document on the 'anycollege' site called 'list of courses', it is necessary to know if it is part of the law department section of the site, or the department of history section or if, indeed, it is just part of the 'anycollege' site as a whole, providing a full list of courses for the entire college.

A more narrow way to define 'site' is to say that a site is a clearly distinct collection of materials. That is, although it may be part of a larger site, and although it may have no independence or separate authority, it does have a distinct identity. By this definition, site is the lowest level of the organizing framework within which a document is located. This is the level that provides most information about the context in which a document exists.

Higher levels of organizations are included in the name you give to the lowest level of organization. For example, if an article on human rights law in East Timor belongs to a collection called 'human rights archive' run by the law department at 'anycollege', then the site the document belongs to is 'human rights archive of law department, anycollege'. Site, defined as the lowest level of the organizing framework, has certain key characteristics. It should have a home page that provides information about that site and provides access to an index of materials on that site. A site should have its own title clearly stated on its home page.

S) Search strategy: exploring a website

Because websites differ so much in how they are organized, every new website you come across can be fairly described as an 'unfamiliar research environment' (Basch, 1998: 182). There is a traditional research approach to such environments that can usefully be adapted and applied to websites.

1. Identify the starting point

When you come across a useful document identify the home page of the site it belongs to. Most of those designing websites design them for users who enter through the home page and this is the best starting point for exploration of a site.

2. Identify the boundaries of the site

Scan the URLs of the links on the home page. Determine which links are internal, leading to other items on this site, and which are external, linking to documents at other sites. Follow the main internal links that seem relevant to your work until they either lead outside the service or end in substantive documents or document collections.

3. Identify which parts of the site are relevant to you

You will do this in the process of identifying the site boundaries.

Site and URLs

URLs can provide a lot of information about how a site is organized and how documents are related to each other. Most folders on websites contain an index document that acts as a home page for that folder. To get a good idea of how a site is organized, look at the index pages for the various folders.

www.school.edu/shapes/circles/frisbees.html

The URL above links to a document about frisbees. The document is in a folder called **circles,** suggesting that **Frisbees.html** is part of a collection of documents about circles or objects shaped like circles. To see the index page for that folder, just 'hack back the URL', by deleting the file name, the last part of the address, and going to **www.school.edu/shapes/circles/.**

When a URL ends in a folder name rather than a file name, your browser automatically looks for a file in the folder called **index.html** or **index.htm (htm** is often used as the file extension for a web page instead of **html).** This will usually act as a sort of home page for that folder. Some people use a different

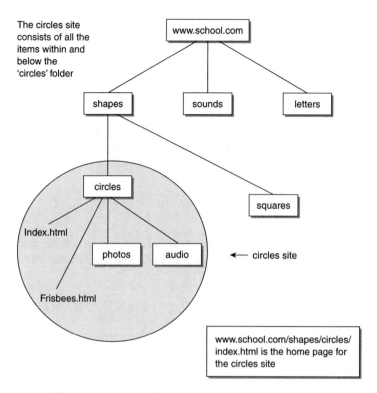

The circles site consists of all the items within and below the 'circles' folder

www.school.com

shapes

sounds

letters

circles

squares

Index.html

photos

audio

← circles site

Frisbees.html

www.school.com/shapes/circles/ index.html is the home page for the circles site

FIGURE 4.5 The structure of a Website

name for the index page in their folder and if you do not get any result using the folder name, you can try adding some of the names commonly used like **default.html, home.html, contents.html** or **toc.html** (table of contents).

If there is no index page in the lowest level folder, go up a level and see if there is one there. In the example given here, try **www.schools.edu/ shapes/,** and if that produces nothing go back up to the domain name **www. schools.edu.**

If you do find an index page in the **circles** folder, you will have to decide if it constitutes the home page of a distinct collection of documents. If it presents itself as a home page or an index page for a site with a clearly stated title, if it provides access to an index of documents connected by a common theme, then it is a site home page, with one important qualification. The documents should be hosted on this site itself, rather than being located on other sites. This is not to say a home page will link only to pages in that site, but its links outside that site are generally external links and it is not the home page for those documents except in rare cases. It will also link to higher levels of the site it is part of.

Exercises

Exercise 1: Exploring academic subject guides

Identify a guide to resources in the broad subject area your research topic belongs to. Use this guide as a starting point to identify at least three other guides in the same subject area.

Use these guides to identify between five and ten key online resources relevant to your research as quickly as possible, including at least one of each of the following:

- A mailing list / discussion list or Blog
- A professional association / scholarly society
- A research centre or institute
- An academic journal

List the titles and URLs of the guides you used. Briefly assess each of these guides. Search at least two of the following search engines using your topic area as your search term (e.g. a search on **"sociology of sport"**).

- Google
- Ask.com
- Yahoo
- MSNSearch

Of the key resources you have identified through the guides, how many of them turn up among the first ten results retrieved in these searches?

Briefly compare the subject guides and the keyword search engines as alternative methods of identifying key resources in a subject area.

Exercise 2: Searching a universal subject guide

Identify a topic of public debate and current interest related to your research topic. Search for guides on the topic in the following services:

- The Open Directory (**dmoz.org**)
- Yahoo Directory (**dir.yahoo.com**)
- Wikipedia (**www.wikipedia.org**)

Briefly describe your experience of searching each of these services.

Assess the quality and usefulness of the guides they provide.

List at least five key resources identified through these guides.

Exercise 3: Analysing web addresses

Identify the URL of a web page relevant to your research. The URL path should include at least two folders after the domain name.

Analyse the URL, explaining what each component tells you about the web page and the site it belongs to.

Hack back the URL and try to identify index pages in each folder and an index page for the domain.

Describe the results of these attempts.

Exercise 4: Exploring a website

Identify a key website in your subject area that is of use in your research.

Explore all sections of the site.

Briefly describe the contents of the site.

List the main section or sections of the site that are of use to you and give the URL for this section or sections.

5
Searching the keyword search engines

Introduction

Many people do all of their Internet searching through the big search engines and it's easy to see why. You'll usually find something useful on your topic reasonably quickly through Google, Yahoo, Ask.com or MSNSearch. There are problems with the search engines, however. It's easy to be swamped with results and it's tempting to resolve this problem by using a few of the items on the first page or two of results even if these are not the highest quality, the most relevant or the most important materials on the subject. It can also be much more difficult to understand and evaluate documents when they are presented out of context as isolated search results.

   You will use the search engines for a range of tasks from the very beginning, but it is best to start systematically searching them only after you have explored the academic literature on your subject and the major online resources in your area through the subject guides. Searching with this experience behind you, you will find that you will already be familiar with many of the sources that appear in your search results and that you will have a much better understanding of the context for the documents your searches pull up. You should also have built up a store of search terms unique to your subject that will allow you to devise specialized queries.

   We tend to think of the search engines as a window on to the Internet but they also play a powerful role in shaping what we see when we search. They give pride of place to paid advertised links, directing us towards commercial services, albeit links clearly marked as 'sponsored' results. The algorithms, the complex mathematical formulae used to decide how to order the search results, often push the most powerful organizations and the most popular sites to the top of the results pages, even though these may not necessarily be the most relevant results. This reinforces the power of the larger sites and ensures that they are far more visible than those on the margins. In this way the search engines can reinforce offline inequalities in power and visibility. When Google complied in 2006 with Chinese government requests to block politically sensitive sites in their new Chinese search service, it provided a stark illustration of the powerful role the search engines play in shaping what we see.

The big four

This section examines in detail the four major search engines – Google, Yahoo, MSNSearch and Ask.com. Google is the best known of the four. There are several other popular search engines but most of them are connected in one way or another with these four. Thus, AOL search and Netscape Search take their search results from Google, while Alltheweb takes its search results from Yahoo. Because these other search engines search the same indexes in slightly different ways, they will pull up different results, but the overlap with the big four is so great that there is little need to search the others separately.

All of the search engines index billions of web pages but it's not possible to directly compare the size of the indexes because they each count the number of items in their index in significantly different ways. Having said this, Google has clearly had the largest index for several years past. Despite their vast size, none of the search engines comes close to covering the entire Web. There is a huge overlap between the search engine indexes, but all of them include millions of results not available in any of the others. If you are carrying out a 'needle in the haystack' search, it is well worth using all four of the major search engines. One of the other big search engines will frequently turn up results for your query that were not available in Google. And because they use different criteria for ranking pages, a search on the same search terms in two of these search engines can retrieve radically different results, despite the massive overlap.

Both Google and Yahoo search Word documents, PDF files, PowerPoint and Excel files and others as well as web pages. The simple search facilities that many websites provide on their own pages often do not search these kinds of files and you can find materials on a website by searching Google that you will not find by searching the site directly.

All of the search engines make some attempt to group together results that come from the same website or domain name. In MSNSearch, the link in a search result to 'more results from . . . ' will pull up all the results from that site that contain your original search term. In Yahoo, the equivalent link is called 'more from this site'. Google and Ask.com group results from the same site together, displaying the first two hits and providing a link to other results from the site.

If you enter more than one word as a search query the search engines treat it as an AND query and will only return documents that contain all of these words. Google will give higher ranking to pages that include your search terms as an exact phrase. The order in which you type search terms will also affect the search results.

The search engines do not distinguish between capital and lower-case letters. If you search for **Snow White** you will get results for both **Snow White** and **snow white**.

Most of the search engines do not provide search 'stemming'. That is, they will search for the exact search term but not for related words using the same 'stem'. If you want results on **child** and **children** you have to enter both terms into the search box. Google provides a limited form of stemming, searching for certain variations on your search terms.

Search Engine Watch (**searchenginewatch.com**) and *Search Engine Showdown* (**searchengineshowdown.com**) provide regular updates on changes to the major search engines and information on studies comparing the search engines.

Google (www.google.com)

Google has become synonymous with searching the Internet, and with good reason. It is the largest of the search engines and it pioneered a ranking system that gives greatest prominence to web pages that a lot of other popular web pages link to. This ranking system is directly modelled on the citation ranking system by which academic journal articles are judged according to the number of other academic articles that cite them. The most linked-to, and often, as a result, the most important, central and significant sites related to a query, come to the top of the results list. This ranking system is not flawless but it can be remarkably effective. Each search result in Google includes a link to 'similar pages'. This pulls up documents with similar linkage patterns. The maximum length for a search query in Google is ten words. Words after the tenth word will be ignored.

Yahoo (www.yahoo.com)

Yahoo has the biggest search index after Google and in recent years has been Google's largest competitor. Yahoo's ranking system assesses both popularity and relevance, just as Google does, but it uses different methods. As a result, it can generate radically different results for the same query. If a page has been included in the Yahoo Directory, Yahoo displays a link to the relevant category.

Ask.com

Search results are ranked according to 'Subject-Specific Popularity'. This is a variation on the system developed by Google. Greater weight is given to links from web pages that are closely related and that are presumably concerned with the same subject matter.

MSNSearch.com

MSNSearch ranks pages according to the relevance of the contents to your search terms and the number of other popular or highly regarded web pages that link to it. It provides a series of advanced search features unique to it. Although it had a notably smaller search index than Google in summer 2006, it clearly aims to compete in the longer term with Google as the most popular search engine.

Advanced searching

All of the major search engines provide an advanced search page. In MSNSearch it's called 'Search Builder' and in Ask.com it appears as an option after you have run an initial search. Many of the options on the advanced search pages can be entered directly into the standard search boxes if you know the equivalent search terms. The following features are available in all of the major search engines, unless stated otherwise.

Search for the exact phrase

You can do this in the standard search box by using quotation marks (e.g. "outrageous assault"). This is the single most powerful way to make your query more precise.

Restrict by language

If you use English language search terms, the overwhelming majority of documents you pull up will be in English. It's not necessary to exclude other languages unless you find there is a confusingly large number of non-English hits. If you're searching for documents in another language, however, you'll often find your search terms pull up a large number of English-language documents which happen to contain your search term for some reason, simply because such a huge proportion of web documents are in English. In this case, it can be useful to limit your search to the language you are interested in.

Restrict by date

Yahoo and Google allow you to restrict your search to materials updated during the last three months, six months or year. If you are running a specialized query again several months after you first searched, this can be useful in excluding some of the results you picked up in earlier searches but it is of limited value. If you limit the search to the last three months, you will pick up plenty of documents that are one or two years old, presumably because some minor element in these pages has been changed in the meantime. Ask.com provides the most sophisticated options, allowing you not only to restrict your search to items updated in the last week or weeks, but also allowing you to limit it to documents updated during a specific time period. If you're researching an event, you can restrict your search to materials that were indexed by the search engine in the few days surrounding that event.

Displaying results

Search engines generally display ten results per page. Google and Yahoo allow you to display up to a hundred results per page. You sacrifice some detail in the results but as you become familiar with your subject area you won't need as much detail. Sometimes you will be searching not for a single document but for all occurrences of a particular phrase. In these cases you may well be interested in all of the results returned, and this option will allow you to move much more quickly through the results.

Restrict by location

MSNSearch has added geographical tags to all of the web pages in their index to allow you to limit your search by country/region. This is a much more effective way of restricting your search geographically than limiting your search by site/domain. Restricting your search to the top-level domain of a particular country does not limit your search to websites operating from that country because so many people register their sites in domains other than those of the country in which they're based.

Adjusting the ranking criteria

This allows you to alter the way in which your results are ranked. It is available only in MSNSearch. You can increase the weight attached to a site's popularity, for example, and reduce the importance attached to how recent it is, by changing a simple sliding scale (see Figure 5.1).

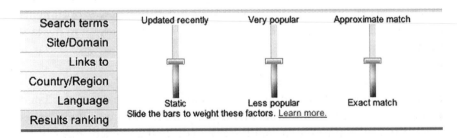

FIGURE 5.1   MSNSearch results ranking options

File formats

Yahoo and Google allow you to restrict your search to certain file formats. You can limit your search to PDF documents (the format used for many published articles and reports), Word documents (used for many course outlines and bibliographies) or a range of other formats.

Restrict by site/domain

This allows you to restrict your search to documents from a particular site or domain. The more detail you provide the more restricted your search. You don't need to use the advanced search page for this. Simply add **site:** to your query. Thus, **site:edu** restricts your search to US universities; **site:harvard.edu** restricts it to web servers at Harvard University; **site:www.ksg.harvard.edu** restricts it to documents on the Kennedy School of Government server at Harvard. Note that you can only include parts of the domain address and can't include any part of the file path. To include the file path, use the **inurl** option outlined below.

Searching URLs

This option allows you to limit your search to URLs. You might search for URLs that include **anthro,** for example, in the knowledge that this is a common abbreviation used in the URLs of anthropology departments. It can also be used to restrict a site search more tightly than is possible when you limit it by site. In a site search you can limit your search to **www.un.org,** the United Nations domain, but the URL search allows you to include all or part of the URL, not just the domain name. It allows you to search for **www.un.org/documents**, limiting your search to items in that particular folder on the UN site. MSNSearch does not provide this as an option in the advanced search but all of the search engines allow you to carry out this search in the normal search box: **inurl:www.un.org/documents**, for example.

Searching titles

You can limit your search to the titles of documents. This is not available as an advanced option in MSNSearch but in all of the search engines you can search titles in the ordinary search box: **intitle:anthology**, for example.

Searching for links

The link search option available in Google and MSNSearch limits your search to documents that link to a particular website or web page. You can also carry out this search by typing **link** in the normal search box. **link:en.wikipedia.org** will return all pages everywhere which link to any document on the English-language version of Wikipedia. **link:en.wikipedia.**

org/wiki/Quaero, on the other hand, returns every page on the Web which links to this Wikipedia entry on Quaero, the European search engine which is intended to rival Google and challenge the domination of American-owned search engines. This search has much in common with an academic citation search. If you find a key website in your area, or a very specialized website concerned directly with your research topic, searching for pages that link to it can provide a unique way of identifying directly related sites.

One specialized search engine, Alexa (**Alexa.com**), will list sites that link to the URL you type in the main search box. It will also indicate the levels of traffic to that site, but only if it's a heavily used site. It is often used to judge the relative popularity of websites.

TABLE 5.1   Advanced search terms

Search term	Examples	Explanation
intitle	**intitle:theory**	Returns documents whose title includes the word 'theory'.
site	**site:edu**	Returns documents where the domain name ends in **edu**.
	site:anycollege.edu	Returns documents where the domain name ends in **anycollege.edu**.
inurl	**inurl:psych**	Returns documents whose URL contains 'psych'.
link: (in Google, MSNSearch and Yahoo)	**link:anycollege.edu**	Returns documents which contain a hyperlink to a page whose URL includes **anycollege.edu**. In Yahoo you have to include **http://** at the start of the address.
	link:anycollege.edu/ pol/index.html	Returns documents which contain a link to this exact URL.

 Search tip: an advanced search using link and site:

To find documents which link to the Boing Boing Archive except for those on the Boing Boing site: **link:boingboing.net/archive.html -site:boingboing.net**

Comparing the search engines

Researchers regularly compare the performance and size of the major search engines. Both **Searchenginewatch.com** and **Searchengineshowdown.com** provide articles on a wide variety of recent comparison studies. Table 5.2 compares the number of hits returned by the major search engines on a series of common phrases in April 2006. It provides a consistent picture of significant differences in scale between the four search engines. Google is well ahead of the rest of the pack, while Yahoo and Google stand out from their nearest competitors. Despite the differences in scale, the smaller search engines include results that neither Google nor Yahoo include. And size isn't everything. If you only need three or four good results, the most important thing is that they come to the top of your search results. It doesn't really matter if the long tail of unused results contains 10,000 or 40,000 hits.

TABLE 5.2   Total hits on a series of common phrases (in thousands, April 2006)

	Google	Yahoo	MSNSearch	Ask.com
"descent into chaos"	84	41	9	6
"blurred boundaries"	86	33	10	8
"atrocious conditions"	78	50	13	10

Meta search engines

Meta search engines run your query on several search engines at the same time so you don't have to waste time visiting each of them individually. Since all search engines have slightly different search syntax, some of the meta search engines simplify, crudely translating your query for search engines that don't understand it. Thus, you cannot be as precise as you can when you go to a search engine directly.

Some of them also include a wide range of specialized databases in their search, emphasizing that they reach into parts of the 'invisible Web' that are not reached by the major search engines. Most of these vast databases have nothing to do with academic research and simply generate a confusingly large volume of results. Some of the best known of the meta search engines are listed below.

Beaucoup (**www.beaucoup.com**)   This allows you to search a wide range of specialized databases and the big search engines simultaneously.

Dogpile (**www.dogpile.com**)   This allows you to do a custom search, specifying which search engines you'd like to search, and in what order. Dogpile shows you how it has altered your query for each search engine.

Metacrawler (**www.metacrawler.com**)   This allows you to search the major search engines. It eliminates duplicates and you can organize results by top-level domain.

Search Allinone (**www.searchallinone.com**)   This carries out joint searches of several major search engines. It doesn't simplify queries as much as some of the other meta search engines do.

Comparing search engines with meta search engines

Tables 5.3 and 5.4 illustrate the results of a 'needle in the haystack' search in all of the major search engines and meta search engines. Because the search turns up so few results, it allows us to examine in detail the overlap between the different search engines. The search, for "**CO 730**" **Archives Iraq mandate** was carried out in April 2006. "**CO 730**" is the code for a British National Archive file on the British government mandate in Iraq in the 1930s. Relevant results are those that deal with the mandate and refer to this specific archive file.

Google returns the largest number of relevant results and includes both of the relevant results found by MSNSearch and Yahoo. In this example, Google completely subsumes the other search engines but you will frequently find results in the other search engines that Google has not picked up in a search like this.

If you run this same search in Amazon.co.uk, Google Book Search and Google Scholar (see Chapters 2 and 3), you will find several results that

TABLE 5.3   Results from major search engines

Search engine	Total results	Relevant results	Overlap of relevant results
Google	9	7	Two were found in Yahoo and MSNSearch
Yahoo	3	2	Both results were found in Google and MSNSearch
Ask.com	0	0	
MSNSearch	3	2	Both results were found in Google and Yahoo

TABLE 5.4   Results from meta search engines

Search engine	Total results	Relevant results	Overlap of relevant results
Beaucoup	0	0	
Dogpile	27	2	Both were found in Google, Yahoo and MSNSearch
Metacrawler	20	1	Found in Google, Yahoo and MSNSearch
Search Allinone	5	4	All four found in Google; two found in Yahoo and MSNSearch

didn't turn up in any of the major search engines, emphasizing that all of the search engines miss out on massive chunks of the Net.

Both *Dogpile* and *Metacrawler* brought back large numbers of results because they simplified the query by ignoring the quotation marks around **CO 730**. Despite the large number of total results, they had few relevant results. By contrast, *Search Allinone* maintained the integrity of the search query and returned more relevant results than any of the others. None of the meta search engines brought back any results that couldn't be found by searching the search engines directly and they missed out on several items that were turned up by direct searches. There doesn't seem to be a strong argument for using the meta search engines in academic research, given that research queries will generally be quite specific and complex. In simplifying queries, the meta search engines, with the exception of *Search Allinone*, hinder rather than help specialized searching.

Boolean searching

Named after an English mathematician called George Boole who devised the basic principles on which it is based, Boolean searching is a small set of simple search terms. The main terms are AND, OR, NOT. Most search engines understand these search terms.

In addition, the search facilities on a lot of individual websites and huge numbers of online databases use Boolean terminology. If you learn the half dozen Boolean terms in Table 5.5, you'll be able to use them in lots of situations.

TABLE 5.5   Boolean searching

Search term	Example	Explanation
AND	**Israel AND Palestine**	Documents containing both words
OR	**Israel OR Palestine**	Documents containing either word
NOT	**Israel NOT Palestine**	Documents containing Israel but not containing Palestine
AND NOT	**Israel AND NOT Palestine**	The same as NOT. Some search engines insist on AND NOT
NEAR	**Israel NEAR Palestine**	Documents containing both words but only if they appear within a few words of each other

You can use the **OR** term to search for variations on a word. Search for **Israel AND (Palestine OR Palestinian)**, for example. You can also use it to make a strict AND search a little bit looser: **revolution AND (communist OR socialist)**, for example. In Google you can omit the brackets.

The Boolean terms AND and NOT can be replaced by plus and minus signs in the major search engines, as illustrated in Table 5.6.

TABLE 5.6   Math searching

Search term	Boolean equivalent	Example	Explanation
+	AND	**+Palestine** **+Israel**	Documents including the words Israel and Palestine
–	NOT	**+Palestine** **–Israel**	Documents including the word Palestine but not including the word Israel

How search engines search

When you enter your query into a search engine it does not search the open web. It searches the index of its own colossal database of web pages. This database is constantly updated by programs called 'robots' that trawl the open web, following one hyperlink after another, adding each new document they locate to the database. The robots locate sites for inclusion by following the links in the web pages they have already indexed. If no other web page links to a web page, the search engines cannot find it unless someone sends them an email letting them know it exists. The speed at which they can work is determined by how fast they can send requests and process the documents they get back. After they retrieve the documents there is a further time delay before they are indexed. Given the vast size of the Internet and the fact that documents change regularly, the search engine databases cannot possibly be kept up to date.

The search engines give priority to major sites and to rapidly changing sites such as news sources, but robots may not visit less prominent sites for months on end. In the meantime the site may have changed beyond recognition or have disappeared completely. The out-of-date information will stay in the search engine database until the robot visits the site again. This is the reason why search engines often bring up hits which don't exist and why they sometimes send you to documents that don't actually contain the keyword you used.

Google, Yahoo and MSNSearch results provide a link to 'cached' web pages, allowing you to view the version of the document cached in their database (and possibly several months old) instead of seeing what's currently at that URL. In the case of a fast-changing site, the 'cached' document may actually be the one relevant to your query.

There are many online databases that the search engines don't cover, including databases of academic articles, newspapers and major organizations. The search engines cannot search any site that doesn't want to be searched. When a robot visits a site the first thing it has to do is request a file called *robots.txt*. If this file says robots are refused access, the robot can venture no further into the site.

Since the search engines can't hope to cover the entire web they have adopted a range of techniques to cope with this. In the case of large websites they will often index just a sample of pages and not even attempt to download the whole site. They only index a certain proportion of the full text of longer documents, the first 100k of a web page in the case of Google (roughly 70 pages of text). A large proportion of the web pages included in the Google databases have scarcely been indexed at all. Only their URLs and titles are indexed. The practical implications of these limitations are clear. When you do a 'needle in the haystack' search on the web for a very rare search term, you cannot be guaranteed of finding all uses of that term online, even if you use several search engines.

The fact that search engines often only sample sites emphasizes the importance of identifying the home pages of useful sites and mining them thoroughly yourself. You can't rely on the search engine to have included every page on a site in its index.

Devising search queries

By the time you come to systematically use the big keyword search engines you should already be familiar with the central resources and the core academic literature in your area. Your queries will be very specific, dealing with a range of specialized issues relevant to your topic. By this stage you will also have a well-developed knowledge of your subject area, know more or less what you're looking for in these searches, and have a rich store of keywords uniquely associated with your topic. All of these provide an essential base for effective searching. Start your search with a reality check, asking yourself who might put material related to your search topic online and why. This will give you a much better sense of the kinds of material you're hoping to find.

Flexibility is the key to efficient use of the big search engines. Think of a query as something that you develop and adapt. If your query does not turn up the required results in the first 10 or 20 hits, devise a new query and search again, and then devise another, and another. If the item you're looking for is in the fifth or sixth screen of hits, then effectively your search hasn't found it at all. It will take so long to work your way down to that screen that it is much more time-effective to change your search terms and do a fresh search.

There is no reason you shouldn't quickly run through four or five queries in the space of 10 minutes. You might carry out four or five quick searches without investigating a single link. To do this you need to learn how to quickly assess the potential relevance of links by scanning and analysing the information on the search results page. This involves getting to know the different genres of web page that exist, knowing the key sources in your area, understanding the URLs and having a good knowledge of your subject area.

Aim for a unique combination of words and phrases which is certain to appear in a document directly related to your topic but which could not possibly appear in other documents. It may sound ludicrously ambitious but it's not. If you can find the right search terms, two or three words in combination can be enough to exclude all but a few web pages. So much has been written and published in the English language over time that the language is replete with clichés. The result is that even apparently distinctive phrases occur in tens of thousands of web pages. 'Descent into chaos', for example, is an evocative and distinctive phrase but it is repeatedly used to describe a wide range of conflict situations, from Vietnam to Iraq. Google returns over 80,000 pages with this exact phrase while Yahoo returns over 40,000.

By contrast with this, an unusual combination of just a few words can be unique, even if they are not distinctively associated with the subject matter. The string of words 'pioneered a ranking' appeared in a sentence earlier in this chapter. This phrase did not generate a single result in Google in May 2006.

In the building of search queries certain kinds of words and word combinations are particularly useful. Several of these are dealt with here.

Quotes

To find discussion of a person's work, search for a few words from a frequently quoted phrase. To find a copy of a piece of written work, search for a short distinctive quote from the work. The quote does not have to be meaningful. If you are looking for the full text of *The Communist Manifesto* by Marx and Engels, for example, a search for the best known phrase from this work "**Workers of the World Unite**" will retrieve over 150,000 documents, only a tiny proportion of them copies of the *Manifesto*. If, on the other hand, you search for a meaningless but distinctive string of words from *The Communist Manifesto*, such as "**tale of the spectre**", virtually all of the 500 hits you retrieve give you the full text of the *Manifesto* or parodies of it.

Names

The name of a person associated with a topic in a peripheral way, perhaps as a minor contributor to an event or project, can be extremely effective in locating very specific information, particularly if the person has a distinctive name. A search for "**Lenchen Demuth**", housekeeper to the Marx family, for example, retrieves materials directly concerned with the detail of Karl Marx's private life much more effectively than a search using Marx's own name.

Place names

In certain cases street names, villages, or the name of a particular building will be linked to your topic and to virtually no other topic. Even the most placeless and theoretical topics will often be associated with particular places – where an experiment was carried out, for example, or where an important centre or individual was based. If the place name is obscure, it can act as a term uniquely (or almost uniquely) associated with your subject. Add a broad term connected to your subject area to modify it sufficiently to cut out all the commercial references.

Common place names are less useful. Particularly if it is a large city or town in the USA, it will appear on tens or even hundreds of thousands of web pages. As a result, it may not act very effectively as a filter. The Internet abounds with lists of things organized geographically, lists of consulates or phone companies or shoe shops. Even the smallest country or region is included in dozens of such lists. Nonetheless common place names can very effectively modify a search that is already quite specific.

Subject phrases

Every subject develops a distinctive terminology that you will become familiar with as your research proceeds and which can be used to ensure that search results relate to that subject area.

Search strategy: building a query

An exploration of the way in which *The Lord of the Rings* has been invoked in relation to the 'War on Terror' might begin with a Google search on **"Lord of the Rings" "War on Terror"**. However, this search brings up almost 400,000 results in Google, indicating that this seemingly obscure combination is much more prevalent than you might have expected. The results are hugely bloated because both phrases are also the titles of video games. **"Lord of the Rings" "War on Terror"** -**game** reduces the results dramatically, to around 80,000. Almost all of the links in the first page of results are directly relevant and provide leads to further debate. The search can be further refined by using a term which is directly associated with the drawing of parallels between The Lord of the Rings and the War on Terror. Adding the surname of Viggo Mortensen, an actor in *The Lord of the Rings* films who drew such parallels, and who was at the centre of public controversy as a result, focuses the search very effectively on recent public debates on the parallels. **"Lord of the Rings" "War on Terror" Mortensen** brings back around 600 results. Google's PageRank system ensures that some of the central sites for discussion of this issue turn up in the first screen of hits. The same search in Yahoo turns up around 700 results, also including several directly relevant results in the first ten hits. Only two of the top ten results in each search engine overlap. The word **Mortensen** is not central to the subject at hand but in combination with the other two search terms, is uniquely associated with a specific public debate on the topic.

The first result is an article in the online magazine, *Salon.com*. The link from this article to 'similar pages' does not return a single page. 'Similar pages' assesses linking patterns and this web page contains virtually no links to other web pages. It illustrates the strict limitations of this facility.

Using the **link:** search to find pages that link to this story turns up only three web pages. By contrast, a simple search on the title of the article returns 11 results, suggesting that the link search is far from effective in finding all those pages that make reference to this one.

Restricting your search by site can be used to limit this search even further. Thus **"Lord of the Rings" "War on Terror" Mortensen site:edu** limits it to US university sites and turns up around 60 results. A search limited to UK academic sites (**"Lord of the Rings" "War on Terror" Mortensen site:ac.uk**) brings up only one result.

The key articles and sites identified in these initial searches now provide an excellent starting point for further searching.

Look before you leap

Certain common genres of web page appear frequently when you do searches on an academic topic. They seem tantalisingly relevant to your search but in the end are of no use. Titles, text extracts and URLs in the list of search results can together help you to decide what kind of document the link leads to without clicking on it. As you learn to recognize a wide range of document genres you can scan search results much more quickly and effectively. Among the most common genres are the following.

College course descriptions

There are now millions of course descriptions and syllabi online. They may include reading lists, an outline of topics to be covered, and a few paragraphs about the topic. As a result, they are packed with keywords related to a very specific subject. You can sometimes identify them because they'll have a course code in the title. If not, the URL will often reveal them as course descriptions. Look for course codes, names of faculty/staff and of departments, URLs like: **www.anycollege.edu/econ/Taylor/macro.html** or **www.anycollege.edu/ psych/courses/py101.html**

Bibliographical references

Publishers, booksellers, colleges and libraries all provide documents that consist solely of lists of books. It's easy to see how a long list of books on psychology, for example, could be densely packed with very specific and obscure keywords related to the subject. Once again, a combination of document title and URL will often tell you this with no need for you to check out the document itself.

Link pages

A long list of hyperlinks to sources on an academic subject will include lots of keywords relevant to the topic but may not contain anything of substance.

 Search tip: bookmarking queries

Most search engines will allow you to bookmark your queries. When you have developed a very effective query, bookmark the page of results it brings up. When you go to the bookmarked page a week or a month or a year later, it will automatically run your query again and bring up an up-to-date results page.

Technical difficulties

Contents lists

Many longer web pages begin with a contents list, a set of hyperlinks that point to various sub-sections of the page. URLs in the contents list will include the telltale # (the 'hash' sign). **frisbees.html#red**, for example, will link you to the part of **frisbees.html** dealing with red frisbees.

If you click on an item in the contents list before the whole document has downloaded, you will often be brought back to the top of the page. This happens when the part of the document it links you to has not yet downloaded.

Each time you click on a link in a contents list your browser treats it as a request for a new document even though you just want to go further down in this document. It's usually quicker to scroll through the document. Each request you make for a sub-section of a document appears as a separate item in your history list and therefore as a separate step you have to take if you use the back arrow.

When 'back' doesn't work

You are looking at a web document. You click on back. The same web document appears. If you have not been using a contents list within that document there is one other common explanation of what has happened.

You connected to a web page whose URL has been changed. A page at the old URL automatically redirects you to the page's new location. It may have redirected you so quickly that you did not even notice. If you then click 'back', you will get the redirect page which automatically sends you back to the document you tried to go back from. Use the history list to jump back over the redirect page.

Parasite frames

Webmasters who use frames on their site can force your browser to put their frame on every document you connect to via their site. Thus, 'sinister enterprises' could provide a page of links to a thousand other websites. When you click on those links, whether they be to the United Nations, the Government of India or the Swedish army, those sites will appear within the 'sinister enterprises' frame. Novice users get the impression that 'sinister enterprises' has responsibility for all of these sites. The parasite frame will attach itself to every site you visit during this session.

Escape by returning to the page on the parasite site where you first chose a link to another page. Click on the link you want to go to, hold down the right mouse button and choose 'open link in new window'. The link will open in a new window free of the parasite frame. (Pfaffenberger, 1997: 107)

Understanding error messages

Error 400: Bad request
There is usually a typing error in the URL you have typed in or in the hyperlink you clicked on.

Error 401: Unauthorized
This is often a password-protected page that you can only access if you have registered for the service it is part of.

Error 403: Forbidden
This is usually a page restricted to certain users. For example, a university server might only allow connections from computers in its own domain. No password is required. You will just be refused access if your computer does not have the right IP address.

Error 404: Not found
You have connected successfully to the server but the particular page you requested does not exist, at least not at the URL you have typed. Either you have made a typing mistake in the last part of the URL (after the domain name) or the page has been moved. If you think it has been moved, have a look at the index page of the folder it is in, or at the folder above it to see if you can find a link to it there. For example, if **www.school.edu/shapes/squares.html** brings up this error, look at **www.school. edu/shapes** and **www.school.edu** for clues as to where it has gone.

Error 500: Internal server error.
There is some problem with the server you are trying to connect to. All you can do is try again.

'Host not found'
Either the domain name is wrong (try typing it again) or your computer cannot connect to your DNS server where it looks up IP addresses for servers. If the latter, it may well be there is a problem with your Internet connection.

'Too many connections'
The site you are trying to connect to is overloaded with requests. Try again immediately. If that does not work try again later.

Exercises

Exercise 1: Building a search query

Devise a very specific search query on an aspect of your topic. The query must include at least one exact phrase and one minus sign (or NOT, the Boolean equivalent). You should build this query up gradually, adding new elements in the light of the initial search

(Continued)

results. The query in its final form should retrieve no fewer than three results on Google or Yahoo, of which at least three of the first ten are directly relevant to the topic you're investigating.

For each stage of building the query, briefly describe the following:

- Your reasons for choosing the elements in the query.
- The number of hits retrieved and how many of the first ten are directly relevant.
- The nature of the first ten hits.
- The way in which you use the information in the first ten hits to refine your search further.

Exercise 2: Restricting by date and site

Taking the search query developed in Exercise 1, or a similarly precise query:

- Restrict the query to pages updated in the past three months.
- What difference does this make to the results? How useful is it?
- Restrict the query to pages from US university sites.
- What difference does this make to the results? How useful is it?
- Exclude pages from commercial sites.
- What difference does this make to the results? How useful is it?

Exercise 3: Page rank

Taking the search query developed in Exercise 1, or a similarly precise query:

- Adjust the 'results ranking' settings in MSNSearch's 'Search Builder'.
- How does this change the results?
- How useful is it?

Exercise 4: Comparing the big four search engines

Run the search query developed in Exercise 1, or a similarly precise query on the following search engines:

- Google
- Yahoo
- MSNSearch
- Ask.com

- How much overlap is there between the top ten results in each?
- Compare the relevance of the top five results. Which search engine returns most relevant results in the top five?
- How many of the search engines turned up the single most important result?

Exercise 5: Searching by link

Identify a key web page directly related to your topic. Search for links to this page.

- Search for the title of this page as an exact phrase.
- Compare the results of these two searches.
- Which is more effective in identifying other web pages that make reference to this key web page?

Exercise 6: Searching by title and URL

Use two or three terms associated with your topic to search for:

- web pages whose title contains any of these terms
- web pages whose URL contains any of these terms

Compare the results of these two searches and briefly describe the advantages and disadvantages of searching by title and URL.

6
Interaction, news and multimedia

Interaction

Web 2.0

A famous US court judgment rejecting censorship in the 1990s described the Internet as a 'never-ending world-wide conversation'. This description emphasizes the interactive aspects of the new technologies. The Internet may be used as a way to distribute documents and images more quickly and cheaply than before but the interactive capacities of the Internet are its most distinctive feature as a medium of communication. These interactive capacities are at the heart of fundamental transformations in the way in which we seek and organize information.

In the mid-1990s veteran online researcher Reva Basch conducted interviews with dozens of people who made their living from finding information online (Basch, 1996). Time and again these experienced researchers mentioned in their interviews that the most valuable resource on the Internet was not the big databases but other human beings. Many of the researchers had stories of how a faraway expert in one particular field was able to answer their question more quickly than they could ever have hoped to have answered it by searching the web or the online databases.

Interaction was initially separated out from the rest of the Internet and took place in newsgroups and on email lists. web logs (blogs, as they're better known) have made it easier for readers to add comments to web pages and have played a central role in breaking down the distinction between websites and online interaction. Blogs heralded fundamental changes in the nature of the Internet, making it a far more interactive environment. The emergence of social networking sites such as Bebo (**bebo.com**) and MySpace (**myspace.com**) have made it a simple matter for anyone with Internet access to set up their own complex website and to use it as a focus for interaction with others. These developments have been paralleled by the development of a wide range of new tools that seek to bottle the magic of interaction, to capture the value generated by contact between people. Web 2.0 is used as shorthand to describe a new generation of online services that, among other things, integrate writer and reader, producer and consumer and blur the boundary between both. It can be seen clearly in operation on the Amazon websites, where reader reviews and recommendations now constitute a major component of the service and a powerful research resource for anyone who uses Amazon. 'Conversation is content', as the slogan puts it. Print and broadcast media have also begun to use reader comments as an important part of their content, while even some academic journals have taken an interactive turn, facilitating online discussion and commentary on individual articles they publish.

Blogs

Blogs allow readers to add comments to individual items posted on a blog. The comments then become an integral part of the blog. Many blogs are used as personal diaries, infrequently updated and of little interest to those beyond an immediate circle of family and friends. At the other end of the spectrum are elaborate blogs maintained jointly by several individuals, often involving organizations, and acting as a major central resource in the area with which they are concerned. Bloggers link intensively to other blogs. If you find one good blog in your area it will lead you to others.

Blogs are structured in a way that makes it easy to make regular new additions. Content is constantly displaced and renewed as older material is pushed to the bottom. Partly because bloggers tend to emphasize the current moment, blogs have a high rate of attrition. Bloggers work intently on keeping a blog updated for several months or a few years and then discover they don't have the time to maintain that level of commitment. They stop paying to maintain their account and the blog simply disappears.

One of the most common types of blog is the news blog, focused on current affairs, commenting on news stories in a particular area or from a particular ideological perspective. Many bloggers argue that the distinction between high-quality news blogs and traditional print and broadcast media is now meaningless and that serious bloggers are entitled to the same recognition as print journalists. As newspapers and television stations establish their own blogs, the gap between traditional and new media is narrowing rapidly.

Many blogs focus intently on current events or current developments in a particular specialized academic field, and act as excellent guides to new resources in those fields. They can usefully supplement a good subject guide in the area by providing a way to keep up to date with new developments. You can sign up to RSS feeds to keep in touch with new entries.

Although this is not inherent to the software or to blogging as a practice, a large proportion of blogs are devoted to highlighting and commenting on stories that have appeared elsewhere, in both traditional media and other blogs. As a result, a single and often very specific story in a newspaper or blog or on a TV or radio station can be the subject of comment in thousands of blogs. Each of these blog entries can attract comments in turn from several readers of the blog in question. While many blog entries and much of the comment on those blogs add little to an understanding of the issues covered in stories, some of the comment adds important additional material and perspectives unavailable elsewhere. If your research involves an issue of contemporary controversy, this provides a genuinely novel kind of resource for detailed investigation of the minute detail of very specific issues.

Searching blogs

The major keyword search engines pick up blogs in their searches but there are also a number of specialized services for searching blogs. Blogs as a genre are much more clearly structured than web pages in general. While it can be difficult to identify what site a web page belongs to, it's simple to identify what blog a post belongs to. Search results in the blog search engines include both the titles of individual messages and of the blog they were posted to. This makes it easy to identify the wider context a post is located in. Bloggers add descriptive tags to individual posts and to their blogs, providing a set of subject keywords for every item in the blogosphere.

All of this should make it easy to search for useful, relevant blogs, but it doesn't. The bulk of blogs do not confine themselves to a single subject but deal with a wide range of topics the author is interested in. It's common for two or three different subjects to come up in passing in a single post. In the circumstances, searching by subject can be one of the least productive ways to approach the blogosphere.

Blogs are concerned above all with the current moment, in the same way as newspapers and television news. Bloggers sweep one way and then the other as public debates shift direction. One of the most productive ways to use blogs is to go with this flow, to use the blogs to trace comment on very specific events and debates, organizing your search around key news stories rather than around subject areas. The scale of public debate is so overwhelming that you can only realistically consider tracing a very specific debate. It would be a lifetime's work to trace, for example, any one of the major themes in public debates associated with the September 11 attacks in the USA. It is much more realistic to take a story like the 2005 article in the science journal *Nature* arguing that Wikipedia was not much more inaccurate than *Encyclopaedia Britannica* (Giles, 2005), a claim strongly contested by the latter (Encyclopaedia Britannica, 2006). A search on **Encyclopedia Britannica Wikipedia** brought up around 400 results in the blog search engine *Technorati* in May 2006. Many of them were not relevant to this particular story but limiting the search to blogs with 'a lot of authority' reduced the number to 23. One effect of this restriction was to cut out a lot of private blogs and to bring to the top blogs that enjoy a lot of links precisely because they are a focus for public debate. Virtually all of the hits in this restricted search make direct reference to this story and lead you to the key newspaper and magazine articles that deal with the issue.

Technorati (**www.technorati.com**) Technorati has a number of unique features that take advantage of the clearly structured character of blogs. Search results allow you to link directly to individual posts or to the home page of the blog they belong to. If you 'sort by freshness', Technorati will bring the most recent results to the top of the search, reflecting blogging's emphasis on the current moment. It will bring the most-linked-to posts to the top if you 'sort by authority'.

This can provide a very effective way to exclude personal blogs and to confine your search to blogs which are part of a vibrant wider network and which are more likely to be a site of public debate and interchange.

The Blog Finder allows you to search the short descriptions, titles and tags associated with individual blogs. Because it does not search the full text of posts, your search needs to be broad. This seems like an ideal way to find blogs on a particular subject but it is not particularly effective because so many blogs are an eclectic collection of comments on a wide range of subjects. The Blog Finder allows you to sort blogs by 'most authority' or 'recently updated'. It also shows tags related to your search term, suggesting other keywords that may be useful.

FIGURE 6.1   Technorati

Google Blog Search (**blogsearch.google.com**) Google Blog Search sorts results by relevance but also allows you to sort them by date, bringing the most recent to the top of the search. The advanced search allows you to limit your search to the titles of blogs, to an individual blog, or to posts written by a particular individual. You can also restrict your search very tightly by date.

S   Search strategy: searching blogs

The blogosphere is a tiny proportion of the Internet. A search with 10,000 results in Google or Yahoo might only bring back a few hundred results in a blog search. As a consequence, you need to make your search terms a little broader than you would in a search of the open web as a whole.

To search for discussion on the way in which the Harry Potter books are brought into political debate you might do a broad search on **"Harry Potter" politics**, for example. In Google this brings up 12 million results but in a Technorati search it only brings up around 9,000 results, in a search in 2006. The results are virtually useless, however, since thousands of people make passing reference to these search terms in diary entries on their daily lives. Limiting the search to posts with a 'lot of authority' radically reduces this to around 300 entries. However, the first 10 or 20 posts have virtually nothing to do with the topic. A search on the same terms in Google Blog Search brings back 12,000 entries. They are sorted by relevance but, even here, very few of the first few hits are relevant. This indicates that the query is simply too broad.

A search on **"Harry Potter" "war on terror"** addresses a particular political debate relevant to the wider topic and brings back radically fewer results – around 500 in Technorati and 400 in Google Blog Search. The first page of results in Google is far more useful than that in Technorati, including several directly relevant items that point to discussions of newspaper articles devoted to the topic. You can use the titles of these articles to track discussion of them in blogs. A search on one of them, **"When Harry met Osama"** retrieves 14 results in Google Blog Search and seven in Technorati. Virtually all of these results are directly relevant to the topic and the search has finally identified a focused cluster of relevant blog posts.

Social networking

By allowing people to easily create their own interactive web pages, services such as Bebo, MySpace and several others have generated a sudden increase in the number of people online and the scale of interaction. The private lives of millions of people have exploded into the public realm with dramatic consequences.

The focus of these sites is private lives and personal networks but inevitably they often become a forum for the discussion of current issues. If you are interested in public debate on a very specific topic and are doing a 'needle in the haystack' search, it may be worth checking these sites. Only registered users can search Bebo directly, but you can search all of these sites through the major search engines. Add **site:bebo.com** or **site:myspace.com** to your query to limit the search to these sites. Users of these sites may hide their pages from public view and no search will allow you to search the full contents of these sites.

The social bookmarking site, **del.icio.us** also rests on the idea that communication is itself content. It allows you to explore other people's bookmarks. You can search by keyword to find bookmarked sites on your topic and then look at the bookmark lists of everyone who chose to bookmark that particular site. It's a novel way to explore the other things that people interested in your topic are concerned about. Its usefulness depends on how many people use the service to store their bookmarks and it remains to be seen whether it develops into a useful research tool.

FURL (**www.furl.net**) takes social bookmarking a step further, allowing you to archive websites you bookmark and allowing you to export citations for websites.

Wikis

Wikis take interaction one step further than the blogs. A Wiki is a website that allows viewers to easily edit its contents. The resulting website is the product of a collaborative effort sometimes involving thousands of people improving, correcting and adding. At its worst it involves viewers deliberately including false information in pursuit of their own agenda, as in the case of the political staffers in the USA, who were briefly banned from Wikipedia after it was found that they were adding misleading information about the politicians they worked for and their opponents (Wikinews, 2006).

Wikipedia (**www.wikipedia.org**) is the best known Wiki project (see Chapter 2), but there are also large numbers of specialized Wikis, many of them aimed at building up resources and knowledge-sharing in specific academic subject areas. To limit your search to Wikis in the big search engines, try adding **wiki** or **inurl:wiki** to your search query. Wiki is increasingly being included in the domain names and URLs of Wikis, making the **inurl** search quite effective. A good Wiki in your area can act as a kind of collaborative subject guide, much more detailed than anything produced by a single individual or organization could be.

Postgraduate students

Students working on a thesis or dissertation have always benefited from contact with others around them in the same position, particularly from contact with those working on related topics. People working in the same physical location remain a key source of support but online access to the experience and knowledge of others in the same position is an increasingly important supplement to this. Postgraduate students – Grad students in US terminology – are among the most intensive users of social networking tools and the most active participants in online discussion. Substantial numbers of them, in the USA in particular, have set up personal blogs that often include useful advice on a wide range of issues involved in writing a thesis or dissertation. These blogs can be particularly useful in providing information on the latest software and research resources being used by these students. They are very uneven in their quality and much advice does not travel very well beyond national boundaries because the educational systems can differ so widely, but it may well be worth exploring the Blogosphere to see if there are one or two useful blogs by postgraduate students in your area.

H-Grad (**www.h-net.msu.edu/~grad/**)   Only registered postgraduate students can subscribe to this list. It deals with a range of issues, including teaching, time management, research concerns, computer programs, choosing an adviser, and job-seeking. Some of the material is of universal interest but the heavy American emphasis means that students outside the USA will find that much of it is of limited value. The website provides links to related resources. Members can search the archives of messages.

JISCmail (**www.jiscmail.ac.uk**)   JISCmail lists, the UK's academic mailing list service, includes a wide range of mailing lists catering specifically for postgraduate students in individual subject areas.

Email lists

Despite the rapid development of new social software, mailing lists continue to serve an important function. Distribution lists are used to send materials in one direction only, like the lists that publishers use to send out regular updates on their new publications. Discussion lists act as forums for exchange and debate. Many discussion lists are unmoderated. The list owner plays no role in channelling or directing the discussion that takes place. These lists tend to get rapidly bogged down in flame wars and are of limited use. Moderated lists are lists in which a list moderator, a real human being, plays some role in filtering or editing messages posted to the list. Most moderators do not use a heavy hand, merely stopping abusive and irrelevant email from being posted to the list. Perhaps the most useful lists are those that are very heavily moderated, such as the suite of academic discussion lists under the authority of H-Net (see below).

There are likely to be at least two or three academic email lists dealing with your subject area that you should be subscribed to. There are a few search engines devoted to searching the titles and short descriptions of email lists, but these will turn up a bewildering array of results. It's far quicker to identify email lists by other routes. Ask other people working in the area what lists they use. Check subject guides in your area (see Chapter 4). They usually include the best-known and most active lists. Check the websites of the key professional associations concerned with your subject to see if they provide discussion lists. Check too to see if there is an H-Net or JISCmail list in your subject area.

H-Net (**h-net2.msu.edu**)   H-Net was initially concerned only with history but has broadened out to deal with the humanities in general and with certain areas in the social sciences too. The H-Net lists are one of the most valuable academic resources on the Internet. Each H-Net list has an editor and an editorial board and is controlled almost as tightly as a print publication. Membership of the lists is composed of academics, postgraduate students and other interested groups, such as journalists and librarians. Editors actively contribute to the lists themselves, powering them along and ensuring that the lists never die from inactivity. Even if you don't join an H-Net list, you can access the H-Net website and the sites for individual H-Net lists and search their archives. If you find the right list, the archives can provide a very focused collection of high-quality material in your subject area. Many of the lists have a very strong US emphasis.

JISCMAIL (**www.jiscmail.ac.uk**)   This is a collection of over 2,500 lists serving the academic community in the UK. You can search by keyword for lists of interest to you. You can also restrict this keyword search to lists in a particular subject area, such as the humanities. Alternatively, you can browse the full list of lists. The keyword search does not search the full text of list archives but only the titles and descriptions of lists.

Lurking
The vast majority of list members never contribute anything to a list, not a single question or answer, let alone an eloquent contribution to debate. One survey of list users showed that 83 per cent of them had never contributed anything. Only about 6 per cent had sent more than one or two messages (Kitchin, 1998: 83, citing Kawakami). The typical list subscriber is a 'lurker' who reads but does not contribute.

Making the most of email lists
Email lists need to be used carefully. If you don't ask the right question in the right place you are likely to be met with silence, or abuse. The advice that follows draws in part on 'The art of getting help' by Phil Agre (1996). The first thing to do is to make sure you are in the right place, that is, on a list where people will take your query seriously, consider it appropriate and be in a good position to answer it.

Mailing lists in your subject area can provide a good forum for initial research queries in a specialized area. This does not mean asking questions like 'please tell me everything you know about the German economy', but rather asking questions about the most useful books on your topic or asking whether there are less obvious sources you should be using. If you ask a question that you could easily answer yourself by checking one or two basic sources, you are unlikely to be received sympathetically. The response to new users asking basic questions on email lists is summed up in the terse abbreviated answer, RTM (Read The Manual), or the less polite RTFM. A lot of lists have an FAQ (Frequently Asked Questions), a document that can often run to 50 pages and answers the questions most commonly asked on that list.

Email lists also provide an ideal forum for very specialized research queries. This is one of the functions of a good email list that at its best is almost magical. Finally, give something back. The more you contribute to helping others the more likely it is that others on a list will be prepared to help when you have a query.

Netiquette

Netiquette refers to a set of informal guidelines for avoiding confrontation in online interaction. It can be very easy to alienate people online. Email and the Internet allow instantaneous responses of the kind previously only possible in conversation, where tone and inflection provided a wealth of extra information about the meaning of what was said. Email messages and posts to blogs and websites are often composed carelessly and hastily by the sender and can be misinterpreted by the recipient. Before you send an email or post a comment on a website or a blog, think twice. Never send a message without re-reading it at least once to check content and spelling. Sometimes you will be amazed to read the things you have typed in haste. Think of the tone too. It is easy to sound abrupt and unfriendly in an email. Without being excessive about it, it is important to keep to a polite tone with people you do not know. Sarcasm and irony travel notoriously badly via email. Avoid them. And don't type in capitals. People think you're shouting at them. In contributing to online discussion, be aware that messages you write now may be available online for decades afterwards.

Flames, trolls and pigs

Wendy Grossman, one of the first journalists to write extensively on online interaction, has compared the Internet to the Babel Fish described by Douglas Adams in *The Hitchhiker's Guide to the Galaxy* (1979). This was a tiny fish you could stick in your ear that would instantly translate any language for you. Adams wrote that the Babel Fish, 'by effectively removing all barriers to communication between different races and cultures, has caused more and bloodier wars than anything else in the history of creation' (cited in Grossman, 1997: 195). The flame wars which rage on email discussion lists, blogs and discussion groups illustrate perfectly the point that easier communication is as likely to facilitate conflict as cooperation.

Flames are abusive email messages. They often begin with disagreement in an email discussion that escalates rapidly into mutual abuse, fits of screaming, threats of violence and finally a full-scale flame war that drags other subscribers to the list into the conflict.

Fascinated by flames in much the same way that arsonists are, some mailing list subscribers deliberately try to provoke flame wars. For some it is a form of recreation to post messages that are so provocative, so filled with hate and invective that other subscribers get whipped up into a frenzy. Those who post these messages just to see what reaction they provoke are called 'trolls'. Just ignore them. 'Never wrestle with a pig. You both get dirty, and the pig likes it,' as one Net saying puts it (Grossman, 1997: 108).

Mailing list search engines

Search engines which search only for lists do not provide the best way to identify key lists in your area because they generate so many results and include vast numbers of dead or dying lists. Once you have identified the key lists in your area by other means you can check these search engines to see if you have missed out on any major lists. Look for lists with large numbers of subscribers. Descriptions of lists can sometimes be inaccurate or too short to be informative.

CataList, the official catalog of LISTSERV lists (**www.lsoft.com/catalist.html**) This only includes lists that use the LISTSERV software. It responds best to simple searching, the broadest terms and every variation on those terms. If it is matters Scottish you are interested in, for example, be sure to search for Scot, Scots, Scotland, Scottish and any other variation you can think of. Each will bring up a different set of results. A huge proportion of lists use this software and CataList provides the best searchable database of these particular lists, one that, according to them, is kept constantly updated. It searches the titles and short descriptions of lists and you can arrange lists by the number of subscribers they have. It also tells you if lists are archived on the web. It seems only a small minority are.

Lists to avoid

Avoid lists that are dead or dying. Since only a tiny proportion of list subscribers ever contribute, it stands to reason that a list with fewer than 100 subscribers is likely to have very little traffic. Constantly active discussion lists by contrast will generally have over 1,000 subscribers and you will usually discover that there are quite a limited number of such discussion lists in your area of interest. Avoid private lists too. These are lists set up by an organization or group of individuals connected by work or a cooperative venture of some kind. Membership is restricted to those at the organization concerned or actively involved in the venture. They were never intended to be publicized at all.

Discussion groups

Messages to discussion groups are posted to the groups online. As a result, messages are archived and easily searchable, unlike the messages in email discussion lists. The keyword search engines do not search the archives of discussion groups and many 'needle in the haystack' searches might turn up something in the groups that wasn't available anywhere else.

As with email messages, the best search strategy is to identify one or two key groups directly relevant to your interests. You can do this by searching the titles and short descriptions of groups using very broad search terms. Alternatively, you can search the discussion group archives to locate references to very specific terms in individual messages.

When searching discussion groups be aware that these posts are much more casual items than web pages or even blogs. They are often written in haste, words are frequently misspelled, abbreviations are used and language is often very casual. This has an impact on the kind of search terms that are most useful.

It is a simple matter for anyone with Internet access to set up a group of their own in either Google or Yahoo Groups.

Google Groups (**groups.google.com**)   Google Groups began when Google took over the running of the Usenet Newsgroups, one of the oldest forums for online interaction. The Usenet archives available through Google Groups include over a billion messages and date back to 1981. Many non-Usenet groups have subsequently been added to Google Groups.

To limit your search to the titles and descriptions of groups, go to 'groups home' where you can also browse through groups organized by subject category. All of the groups returned in the search results are grouped according to subject area, language and activity levels, making it a simple matter to identify the largest groups in your subject area. You can limit your searches to individual subject categories when you search the full text of posts.

When you do an ordinary search in Google Groups, searching the full text of posts, the results list will be headed by groups that match your search term. The other results show a group name, a brief description of the group and the subject category it belongs to. They also provide links to a full list of discussions in groups that include your search term. These discussions consist of all of the individual messages that belonged to a particular discussion.

In the advanced search you can limit the search by author, allowing you to trace the posts of an individual contributor. When you post messages to discussion groups you are laying out a trail of opinions which can be followed by others years later. You can also limit your search very tightly by date. If you are interested in a particular event, this allows you to focus in on the interaction that took place immediately after the event. The advanced search also allows you to sort results by date or by relevance.

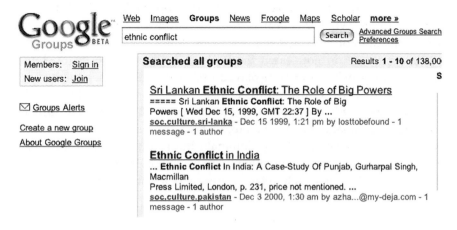

FIGURE 6.2   Google Groups search results on ethnic conflict

Usenet hierarchies in Google Groups

Usenet Newsgroups had their own system of hierarchical ordering according to subject category before they came under Google's wing. Subsequently, thousands of additional groups have been added to Google Groups but have not been slotted into the Usenet hierarchies. Instead, Google has created a new system of categorizing groups by subject. A huge proportion of the Google groups are still part of that Usenet hierarchy, however, and understanding it can help you to identify relevant groups.

Below is a list of some of the top-level Usenet hierarchies relevant to the social sciences and humanities:

- Alt – alternative
- Comp – computers
- Misc – miscellaneous
- Rec – recreation and hobbies
- Sci – science
- Soc – society, culture, religion
- Talk – discussion, focused on current issues

Each of these is home to hundreds or even thousands of individual newsgroups. The top level of the hierarchy is the first part of a newsgroup name. For example, **soc. culture** belongs to the soc hierarchy. It is for discussion of culture in general. **soc.culture.indian** also belongs to the soc hierarchy and is for the discussion of Indian culture. **soc.culture.indian.kerala** is for discussion of the culture of the Indian state of Kerala. There are also top-level hierarchies specific to certain regions, including **de** (Germany) **au** (Australia) and **uk** (United Kingdom) that provide groups which will be of interest to users dealing with these particular areas or countries.

Yahoo Groups (**groups.yahoo.com**)   Yahoo Groups are organized into subject categories. When you search in Yahoo Groups to 'find a group', you search the titles of subject categories, and the titles and long descriptions of the groups. You do not search the full text of messages. Categories that match your search term are displayed first. The subject categories are not particularly useful because a broad category, such as Geography, includes huge numbers of local groups targeted at a particular research group or a particular set of students, for example. These groups are of minimal value to a wider audience and they dominate the results in some categories. Search results show you how many members each group has but it is not as easy to limit your search to larger groups as it is in Google Groups.

S   Search strategy: searching discussion groups

A search for discussion on the way in which the Harry Potter books are invoked in political debate might start with the query that proved useful in searching blogs. In Google Groups **"Harry Potter" "War on Terror"** identifies the main forums for discussion on this topic, bringing back five groups which include posts with these search terms, among them **alt.fan.harry-potter** and **alt.politics.liberalism**. Information on the numbers of subscribers and the levels of activity indicate that these are heavily used groups. The links to posts reveal lively debate in these groups on this precise topic.

This very specific query has been useful in identifying the main groups relevant to any discussion of politics and the Harry Potter books. Further searching can be limited to these two groups and can take very different forms. In **alt.politics.liberalism** searches can draw entirely on terms related to the Harry Potter books, while in **alt.fan.harry-potter** political search terms will produce the most useful results.

This search is much less productive in Yahoo. **"Harry Potter" "War on Terror"** returns no results while a search on **Harry Potter** turns up lots of groups, none of which seems any more likely than the others to include political discussion.

News

Current news is available in vast quantities all across the Web, searchable by keyword and by topic. The big online news services, such as Yahoo News (**news.yahoo.com**), Google News (**news.google.com**) and MSN Newsbot (**newsbot.msnbc.msn.com**), draw on a wide variety of newspapers,

TV and radio stations and wire news services for their content. They include audio, video and text. Google News, for example, draws on over 4,500 news sources. There is a huge overlap in the coverage of these big services. Google News gives prominence to a much more diverse array of news sources from across the globe, partly because the news page is generated automatically, without human intervention. As a result, American and British news sources are not as prominent as they are in Yahoo News. MSN Newsbot services are tailored to audiences in different countries.

The advanced search options of both Yahoo News and Google News allow you to restrict your search to individual news sources, or to particular countries or regions. Yahoo News also allows you to limit your search to broad subject categories, such as politics or health. All of the services are extremely shallow in terms of time. Google News and Yahoo News allow you to search through news stories from the previous 30 days only. To get greater depth you need to go to the news archive databases.

RSS: really simple syndication

RSS has become a popular way of keeping up with news without having to regularly return to the relevant web pages. An RSS feed provides you with short summaries of the stories currently available at a particular web page and links directly to the stories themselves. RSS readers make it easier to organize information from all of the sites you return to regularly. RSS and Atom are two of the most common formats for delivering such feeds.

Lexis-Nexis (**www.lexisnexis.com**) LexisNexis provides the full text of articles from thousands of newspapers. You can restrict searches to publications from particular countries, or to individual publications. A 'source directory' lists the different publications that are available. Partly because they have been in the online database business for so long, LexisNexis has the deepest historical coverage of several major British and American newspapers. It is only available if your university or library subscribes to the service.

LexisNexis Alacarte (**alacarte.lexisnexis.com**) This is aimed at users who do not have access to LexisNexis. You pay per document for stories from over 20,000 news sources dating back to 1968. You can select a number of publication titles and search them jointly or limit your search to a single publication. You can restrict your search by date and restrict it to certain kinds of sources.

News Library (**www.newslibrary.com**)   This is an archive of articles from more than 800 newspapers, heavily weighted to US material and including large numbers of local and regional newspapers in the USA. Coverage in terms of time varies greatly from one newspaper to the other. Flexible search options allow you to search one or all or any combination of newspaper titles in the archive. Anyone can search for free and retrieve the first paragraph of an article but if you want to see the full text you have to pay. It also searches transcripts of television and radio programmes and the archives of some wire services. The advanced search allows you to limit your search to headlines or to the first paragraph of a story. The first paragraph usually distils the content of the entire article ('Who's gonna read the second paragraph?' as the editor said to the reporter in *The Front Page*, a classic 1931 film about the newspaper business).

ProQuest News & Magazines is one of the databases provided by ProQuest, which also produces databases of academic articles. If your institution is a subscriber, there should be a link from your library's website. It covers over 1,400 newspapers and magazines. Records for most papers go back no further than 1986 but this gives the database a greater historical depth than some others. Information from the larger newspapers can be on the database within 24 hours of publication.

The bulk of newspapers and magazines have websites that provide access to their own archives. In some cases they simply provide another route to the archives held in the databases listed above. The archives of individual newspapers can in some cases be more complete and are searchable in very different ways from the articles from those papers which form part of larger databases. It can sometimes be difficult to find your way to the archive of a newspaper from its website. Because of the focus on the present moment, archives are often buried deep within the websites and you may need to do a little digging to find them.

The sites listed below maintain large collections of links to the websites of individual newspapers, magazines and broadcast media.

- *Internet Public Library List of Newspapers* (**www.ipl.org/div/news**)   Links are organized geographically and are searchable by keyword.
- *Newslink* (**www.newslink.org**)   Links to newspapers, magazines and broadcast media provided by the *American Journalism Review*.
- *Yahoo: News and Media Category* (**dir.yahoo.com/News_and_Media/**) This guide links to a huge variety of news sites, organized by media type, by subject, and by country.

These listings usually make little attempt to distinguish between newspapers of record, which emphasize accuracy and the ideal of objective reporting, and newspapers which place less emphasis on these ideals. If you are looking for newspapers from a particular country, a better starting point can often be a general Web guide to resources on that country, which will almost always include annotated links to that country's media. Many newspapers charge fees for full access to their archives, although you can often conduct searches and read extracts from articles for free.

Wire services

Wire services, such as AFP, PA and UPI, have become a principal source of news information on the Web because even before its advent they were geared up to rapid and flexible worldwide delivery of news. Most newspapers have taken stories from these services for decades, using them for coverage of countries where they themselves could not afford to have a full-time reporter. Now the wire news feed which once came into the offices of newspapers is available to anyone through the Web, and the wire services have made deals to provide searchable up-to-date news via almost every search engine, portal and news site on the Internet. Below is a list of some of the major wire services.

* AFP: *Agence France Press*, France (**www.afp.com**).
* AP: The Associated Press, US (**www.ap.org**)   You can search news from the previous seven days, including photos, video and audio. You can search the archive for free and buy the full text of articles going back to 1998 (**www.newslibrary.com/sites/apab**).
* China View: Xinhua online, the Chinese government news agency (**www.chinaview.cn**).
* PA: Press Association, UK (**www.pressassociation.co.uk**)   This service is aimed primarily at serving journalists and the media.
* Reuters, UK (**today.reuters.com/news/**).
* TASS, Russia (**www.itar-tass.com/eng**).
* UPI: United Press International, US (**www.upi.com**).

You will find news reports all over the Internet, placed by individuals on their websites or blogs, or forwarded by email. Beware of news items presented as second-hand. Always try to find the official version. It is a simple matter for someone to crop or alter a text to suit their own purposes before they forward it or put it on the web.

Multimedia

Visual and audio resources have not been heavily used in research in many social science and humanities disciplines. One reason for this was the inaccessibility of these resources and the lack of specialized technical knowledge. The Internet has made it a much simpler matter to locate and to manipulate images and sound. Some of the biggest broadcasters have begun to experiment with making a wide range of film clips, audio clips and images available for free under a variety of 'creative commons' licences, which allow people to use these copyright materials under certain conditions. One of the leaders in this is Britain's BBC (**www.bbc.co.uk**). Materials are often made available on condition that the original author is acknowledged and that they are not used for commercial purposes. It is now a much simpler matter for a research student to use video and audio clips as well as a wide range of images in a thesis or dissertation.

In addition, there has been a dramatic increase in the multimedia resources made available through 'social networking' or Web 2.0 services. Among the most popular things for people to share and publicize through these sites are the videos, images and sounds they themselves have produced. In some cases these services have effectively become massive new public libraries full of multimedia resources, many of which can be used by anyone.

Many web pages and websites incorporate a wide range of media, mixing video clips with images and animated graphics, and there is no clear boundary between print and audio and visual resources online. However, there are a number of services devoted specifically to locating non-text resources.

Images

Image searches are available in Google, Yahoo, Ask.com and MSNSearch. Because these image searches search a very small amount of text, you need to use broad search terms rather than the very specific queries you use to search the full text of documents. Because images are often not clearly labelled, you may need to try a variety of search terms related to your topic. If a keyword search turns up one image relevant to your search, you can go to the web page where the image is imbedded to see if it is part of a wider collection of related images.

Photo sharing websites provide an additional source of images online. Several such sites, including Flickr (**www.flickr.com**), Webshots (**www.webshots.com**) and PBase (**pbase.com**), contain millions of photographs posted by individual users. Many of the photographs on these sites are restricted to certain viewers while many others are available for a fee, but a huge proportion of the photographs are freely available to anyone. If you use photographs from these sites you need to credit photographers and ensure that you are entitled to use the photos. These collections do not overlap to any great degree. If you are searching for a very specific image it is well worth searching all of them.

The best known of these sites is Flickr (**www.flickr.com**). Flickr provides an illustration of several features that are common to many of these sites.

Individual photographers add descriptive 'tags' (keywords) and sometimes short descriptions to their photographs. The advanced search (**www.flickr. com/photos/search**) allows you to search for one or more tags or to simultaneously search titles, tags and descriptions of the photographs.

Results are organized into clusters that group pictures according to the broad themes suggested by the other tags used to describe them. This can very effectively sort the results by theme and can also suggest related tags that it might be useful to search on.

You can use individual photographs to guide you to relevant collections by exploring the collections of the photographer. In addition, Flickr users have created pools, collections based on a common theme, to which large numbers of people can post their images. Individual images can lead you to pools of related images and you can sign up for regular updates on new additions to these pools.

There are also large numbers of commercial image banks and stock photography services that allow users to search massive collections of images, some of them royalty-free, others for sale. You will find a wide range of these services by searching a search engine for **"image bank"** or **"stock photography"**.

The UK academic service, Image Sites database (**www.tasi.ac.uk/ imagesites**) includes hundreds of specialized image collections, including almost 200 collections of historical images. You can browse by subject or search by keyword. It is focused on the UK.

One major source of images online remains inaccessible to the general public. Some of the biggest media companies which sell images to newspapers, magazines and design professionals still don't make these huge image banks easily and cheaply available to the general public.

 Search strategy: searching for images

Flickr is particularly strong on contemporary images and a search for historical photographs of the Berlin Wall on Flickr yields relatively little. **Berlin Wall** returns recent photos of the pieces of wall that remain, but few historical photographs. The Berlin Wall came down in 1989 and a search on **Berlin Wall 1989** retrieves over 50 photographs, most of them dealing with the fall of the Wall, but only a few of them portraying the Wall before its demolition. The photographs suggest a few other tags to use in the search but none of them are particularly useful.

(Continued)

By contrast a search in Google Images on **Berlin Wall 1989** brings back over 700 results. Because there are so many results, the search can be narrowed considerably. **Berlin Wall 1988** shifts the emphasis away from the year in which the Wall was destroyed in an attempt to get older images. It brings back 80 results. The first few pages of hits include historical photographs of the Wall that belong to extensive archives of relevant photos.

The Yahoo Images search returns over 60 results for **Berlin Wall 1988** and points you to several collections of historical photos that didn't turn up in the first few screens of the Google search. By this stage the search has identified several useful collections.

But these image search engines do not necessarily provide the only way or the best way to identify collections of images. A simple search in a conventional search engine such as Ask.com on **Berlin Wall 1988** turns up links to a few major archives of historical photos of the Berlin Wall that didn't appear in the early results of any of the image searches. If you do your image searching using the ordinary search engines, you can be much more specific than you can when using the image search facilities. **Berlin Wall photographs historical archive** brings up nothing in Google Images or Yahoo Images but in Google it brings up a huge variety of results, including links to several websites providing historical photographic archives of the Berlin Wall.

Maps

Images of maps from a wide range of sources are available on the image search engines listed above and on the photo sharing sites. Adding **map** to your query will narrow your search very effectively in all of these services. You will often find that the same map is available online at many different locations. In these cases you need to track down the original source in order to find out which organization or individual produced the map and to credit them accordingly.

One of the largest online map collections is the *Perry-Castañeda Library Map Collection* (**www.lib.utexas.edu/maps**). It also provides a guide to other map sources online. There are several weblogs devoted to online maps. One of the most prominent is *The Map Room: A Weblog About Maps* (**www.mcwetboy.net /maproom**).

More recently, Google maps (**maps.google.com**) and Yahoo maps (**maps.yahoo.com**) have begun to open up a wide range of new possibilities for online maps. Large numbers of individual users have begun to create their own specialized maps to display data such as crime figures or property prices using Google maps. These are referred to as mashups. Several blogs are devoted to covering the latest developments in Google maps and online mapping in general, among them Google Maps Mania (**googlemapsmania.blogspot.com**).

Video

Over the past few years, hundreds of thousands of individuals have put their own video footage online, using new technologies for videocasting (video podcasting) and vlogging (video blogging). In addition, television stations, academic institutions and a wide variety of commercial and non-profit organizations have begun to make video materials, and video archives, much more freely available online. While video online is dominated at the moment by the amateur and the private, the Internet is quickly becoming a means for distributing mainstream video resources too, including films and television programmes. As broadcasters begin to make mainstream television programmes available online for free or at a minimal charge, the distinction between television and the Internet is being steadily eroded.

Because programmes that have been broadcast on television include 'closed captions', you can search the full text of these broadcasts, if they are available online. Note that closed captioning is not always completely accurate. For video that hasn't been broadcast you are limited to searching titles and the short descriptions or keywords provided by those who produced them.

The Moving Image Gateway (MIG) (**www.bufvc.ac.uk/gateway**) is maintained by the British Universities Film and Video Council (BUFVC). It acts as a guide to over 600 online resources relevant to the use of audio and video materials at university level. You can browse by subject or search by keyword. The UCLA Arts Library provides a guide to *Selected Internet Sources in Film* (**www.library.ucla.edu/libraries/arts/websites/wwwmov.htm**) that includes other online guides, film archives and relevant databases.

One rich source of freely downloadable films is the Internet Archive's *Movie Archive* (**www.archive.org/details/movies**). It includes archive documentary films, propaganda films and films that have gone out of copyright.

Academic video resources have also become much more freely available online. *ResearchChannel* (**www.researchchannel.org**), a 'Social Sciences Video and Webcast Library' established by a consortium of US universities and libraries, provides access to video of over 3,000 academic events and lectures. It is heavily focused on US politics and international politics. It also provides advice on educational use of these materials.

Among the most common genres of video material available online are movie trailers, music videos, personal home video, videos produced by political organizations, video of protests and public events, and archive footage. Some of the search engines also pick up video clips hosted on the websites of television stations. You can do a much more comprehensive search of these stations' output by searching them directly. You can find the websites of most television stations by simply typing the station's name into one of the big keyword search engines.

Among the major video search engines are:

- *Google Video* (**video.google.com**)
- *Yahoo Video Search* (**video.search.yahoo.com**)
- *Singing Fish* (**search.singingfish.com**) (also searches audio materials)

A number of services allow individuals to place their own videos online. Among the best known are:

- *YouTube* (**www.youtube.com**)
- *IFILM* (**www.ifilm.com**)
- *Vimeo* (**www.vimeo.com**)

Video weblogs, or vlogs, are distinguished from the video sources listed above because they are presented as a kind of online TV series in the same way that many podcasts are presented as a kind of regular radio show. Among the major sources for locating these vlogs are:

- *FireAnt* (**fireant.tv**)
- *Videoblog directory* (**mefeedia.com/feeds**)
- *VlogDir, the Videoblog Directory* (**vlogdir.com**)

Audio

Many radio stations make audio files of their broadcasts available online, including material from their huge archives of news and documentary programmes. You can also listen online to the current output of a huge proportion of the world's local and national radio stations, over 5,000 of them broadcasting online. You can find most stations easily by searching for the name of the station, and its location if necessary, in one of the keyword search engines.

When you search these sites for audio files you are generally searching short text descriptions of the files and your search terms need to be correspondingly broad. More recently, it has become possible to automatically generate text files from audio files, allowing you to do full-text searches within the content of files. This will allow much more precise searching of audio materials but this technology is still in its infancy.

CADENSA is the online catalogue of the British Library National Sound Archive. You can search this database of over 2.5 million recordings but you have to visit the Library if you want to listen to them (**www.bl.uk/collections/sound-archive/cat.html**). *National Public Radio* in the USA provides a free online archive of thousands of hours of their programmes, including news broadcasts (**www.npr.org/archives**).

Podcasting

Podcasting provides an easy way for people to make their own audio recordings available online. The new technology has sparked a rapid increase in the variety and number of audio materials available online. Many of the podcasts have a very experimental and amateur character. If podcasts become significant to people researching your topic, they should begin to feature in subject guides or discussion lists in your area. This might provide a quicker way to identify useful materials than searching the podcast search engines dealt with below.

However, because so many podcasts are ephemeral, the guides may not pick them up. It can also be useful to search for them by searching blog search engines, searching for **podcast** and the appropriate keywords. If a significant interview or statement or resource has been made available by podcast, it may have been picked up by the bloggers who comment on current affairs, even if it never made it into a subject guide.

Podcasts are modelled on radio shows. A podcast series consists of a number of episodes. You may identify a useful series or a short extract from a particular episode that deals with your topic. Huge numbers of podcasts are locally focused or, like the blogs, deal with an eclectic range of subjects determined by the personal interests of the podcaster.

Yahoo Podcasts (**podcasts.yahoo.com**) Podcasts are organized by subject categories. You can explore the subject categories or search by keyword. The keyword search searches the titles, descriptions and tags associated with podcasts. You can choose to search for series using broader search terms, or to search individual episodes using more precise terms.

Podcast.net: The Podcast Directory (**www.podcast.net**) You can browse through lists of podcasts organized by subject categories, by location and by language. You can also search by location, finding all of the podcasts broadcasting from a specific location. The keyword search searches titles and descriptions.

Apple iTunes: podcasts (**www.apple.com/itunes/podcasts**) You can search and subscribe to podcasts through the Apple Itunes store, which provides sophisticated options for managing podcasts on an iPod.

Exercises

Exercise 1: Searching blogs

Identify a specific news story you are interested in. Search in Technorati and in Google Blog Search to find references to this story. If the first news story you identify turns up no search results, try again with a story that is more likely to have generated online debate.

When you have developed a query that generates useful results, compare the results on Technorati and Google Blog Search.

(Continued)

- How much overlap is there between the first ten results?
- Which of them generates the most useful results? Give reasons for your answer.

Explore one or two of the related tags generated by these searches that seem likely to be useful.

Briefly describe the results and the usefulness of searching on these tags.

List one or two key print articles identified in your blog search.

Use the titles of these articles as search phrases to search again for discussion of the stories.

Briefly describe the results and the usefulness of this search.

Exercise 2: Searching email lists

Find the H-Net list most relevant to your research topic.

Search the list's archives (if possible) using a few broad terms and a few specific phrases related to your research topic. Try searching using the title of a key book in your area. Briefly describe the results of this search.

If it can be done easily, subscribe to the list. Watch the traffic for a few days. Based on this traffic, is the list likely to be useful to you? Explain your answer.

Search for a JISCmail list relevant to your research topic by browsing the subject categories.

Search for a JISCmail list by keyword.

Compare these two methods of identifying a relevant list.

Briefly describe the search process by which you identified a relevant JISCmail list.

Search CataList to find heavily used lists relevant to your topic.

Subscribe to at least three and watch the traffic for a few days. Based on this traffic, are any of the lists likely to be useful to you? Explain why.

If you were asked for advice on how to find a useful list, what would your advice be? (Limit this answer to three or four sentences).

Exercise 3: Searching discussion groups

Use a precise and distinctive query in Google Groups to identify two or three key groups relevant to your topic.

Pick one of these groups and search within the group.

Describe one or two relevant discussions turned up by your search.

How useful are these discussions to you?

Use broader search terms in Yahoo Groups to identify two or three key groups relevant to your topic. Do these groups seem likely to be useful?

Exercise 4: Searching for images

Identify a type of image that would usefully illustrate your research topic. Search for images of this type using the image search facilities of at least two of the following search engines:

- Google
- Yahoo
- Ask.com
- MSNSearch

Use the results to identify collections of related images.

Search for images of this type in at least two photo sharing sites, such as:

- Flickr
- Webshots
- Pbase

Use the results to identify a photographer or a photo pool that provides related images.

Search for images in at least two keyword search engines, such as:

- MSNSearch
- Google
- Yahoo
- Ask.com

Use the results to identify collections of related images.

Describe the process of developing these search queries in each case.

Compare the experience of searching and the search results generated by these different searches.

What is the most effective way to conduct a search for the kind of image you were looking for? Give reasons for your answer.

Exercise 5: Searching for video

Identify a television station likely to provide material relevant to your research. Search and explore the station's website to identify video clips relevant to your research.

(Continued)

Briefly describe the video materials this station makes available, the various methods of searching for them and, in your experience, the most successful search approaches to this particular site.

Search for video clips relevant to your research in at least two video search engines, such as:

- Google Video
- Yahoo Video Search
- Singing Fish

How much overlap was there between the top ten results for the most useful search query you devised? What kinds of material did these searches turn up? How do these materials compare with the materials identified by searching the television station?

Search for video clips relevant to your research in at least two of the following services or in similar services:

- YouTube
- IFILM
- Vimeo
- FireAnt
- Videoblog directory
- VlogDir

How much overlap was there between the top ten results for the most useful search query you devised. What kinds of material did these searches turn up? How do these materials compare with the materials identified by searching the television station?

Exercise 6: Searching for audio

Identify a radio station likely to provide material relevant to your research. Search and explore the station's website to identify audio clips relevant to your research.

Briefly describe the audio materials this station makes available, the various methods of searching for them and, in your experience, the most successful search approaches to this particular site.

Search for podcasts relevant to your research in at least two podcast search engines, such as:

- Yahoo Podcasts
- Podcast.net

How much overlap was there between the top ten results for the most useful search query you devised? What kinds of podcast did these searches turn up? How useful are these podcasts in your research?

7
Governments, archives and statistics

**Niall Ó Dochartaigh and
Patricia Sleeman**

Introduction

Government publications, official archives and data collected by government statistical offices are central to much research in the social sciences and humanities. The Internet has dramatically increased the accessibility of these primary sources.

Like the academic articles and books dealt with in earlier chapters, the resources covered in this chapter are clearly marked off from the open web, and are characterized by well developed and often very complex organizational structures, indexes and classification schemes. To a much greater degree than with any other online resource, it is essential to get to know and understand these sources. Of the thousands of archives, of the millions of collections held by those archives, there might be half a dozen items of use to you and you're unlikely to find them through random keyword searches. The vast quantity of published academic books and articles can often seem overwhelming and impossible to get to grips with because of their abundance. But the deep stores of information held in archives, buried in datasets and in government records, make the academic literature look like a thin analytical skim on the top of a vast sea of information. It is only through the development of expertise in your subject area, through contact with people who know the sources, and through looking at the sources used by others working in the same area that you will develop knowledge of which archives, which statistical resources and which collections of government documents are likely to be of use to you. It's only with that initial direction that you can effectively search these resources online.

Governments

While governments make many of their publications freely available online, and generally provide very sophisticated search options, it can be difficult to find your way through these vast storehouses of documentation. There are often multiple routes to the same materials. Going to a government site and doing keyword searches there is not usually the quickest way to identify relevant government documents.

If you are interested in an issue of current controversy, there are several other routes that are worth trying first. Governments often provide guides to their documentation on current issues and press releases aimed at journalists and an interested public. While these guides are not comprehensive and are often concerned primarily with presenting materials that support the government's case, they can provide a quick introduction to the kinds of official documentation available, suggesting future avenues for searching.

It is useful to supplement this by searching for government documents from the other side of the fence, by using the resources provided by critics of government policy. The workings of government are the direct concern of political activists, non-governmental organizations and elected representatives. All of these have a strong interest in, and knowledge of, government documentation on the issues that concern them.

News stories can also provide a short-cut to government documents. Government policy is the stuff of controversy, debate, dispute and argument, and is therefore the subject of extensive news coverage. News stories can point to the names of key individuals, government reports and key phrases which you can then use as search terms when searching government sources directly.

 Search tip: searching for government information by domain

On Google, Yahoo, Ask.com and MSNSearch add **site:gov** to your query to ensure you only search US government sites. Add **site:mil** to restrict it to US military sites. Note that not all government documents are to be found in the official domains. You can use the same syntax to restrict your search to any domain you choose, and you are not limited to top-level domains. Thus **site:gov.uk** will limit your search to UK government sites while **site:fco.gov.uk** will limit it even more narrowly to the site of the UK's Foreign and Commonwealth Office. To identify the domain name for other governments or government departments, investigate the links in *Foreign Government Resources on the Web* **(www.lib.umich.edu/govdocs/foreign.html).**

In some cases it can be easier and more productive to search government resources via a search engine than to search them directly. A search engine can turn up materials that you'll miss if you search the sites directly. Thus, Google searches the text of PDF documents hosted on government websites while some of these websites don't search their own PDF files – a very significant fact considering that the bulk of published documents placed online are PDF documents.

The British government

In common with many other European governments, the British government has enthusiastically adopted the Internet in the hope and expectation that it will bring government and citizen closer together. The Internet is used to provide detailed information about public services to citizens through *Directgov* (**www.direct.gov.uk**) and to carry out public consultation on government policy proposals. Government publications, records of parliamentary proceedings and government press releases are all available through a variety of overlapping services. Individual government departments provide collections of documents relevant to their responsibilities and there are also several central indexes of government documents.

Key guides include *Official and Government Resources* (**www.britishlibrary. net/official.html**), a guide from the British Library covering governments around the world but particularly strong on British government resources. The Keele University guide to *British Government and Politics on the Internet* (**www.keele.ac.uk/depts/por/ukbase.htm**) includes sections on UK government resources.

House of Commons Library Research Papers (**www.parliament.uk/parliamentary_ publications_and_archives/research_papers.cfm**) A collection of research papers on topics of contemporary political controversy, put together by staff at the British House of Commons Library to provide summaries of fact and opinion on these issues for British Members of Parliament. They can provide a useful introduction to a topic of current or recent political debate.

UK Parliament (**www.parliament.uk**) The advanced search on the Parliament website allows you to restrict your search to particular types of publication. Select 'Commons Hansard' to limit it to the text of proceedings in the House of Commons. Limit your search to 'Select committee report' to search the reports produced by parliamentary committees that deal with government policy. You can also search the Parliament site through a search engine such as Google or Yahoo by limiting your search to

site: publications.parliament.uk. The search engines don't allow you to restrict the search according to the kinds of material you want to search, but search engine results show the text around your search terms, something you don't get if you search the site directly.

Document Type - Which set of pages or document type do you want to search?		
Sections to search:	**Across both Houses**	**Bills**
	☐ Weekly Information Bulletin	☐ Explanatory Notes
	☐ Sessional Information Digest	☐ Bills
	☐ Sessional Returns	☐ Bill Amendments
	☐ Directory	**Committees**
	☐ Information Pages	☐ Committees Home Pages
		☐ Select Committee Report
	Commons	☐ Standing Committee
	☐ About the Commons	
	☐ Questions for Oral and Written Answer (Order book)	**Hansard**
	☐ Commons Written Answers	☐ Commons Hansard
	☐ Summary Agenda and Order of Business	☐ Lords Hansard
	☐ House of Commons Commission Annual Report	☐ Official Report (Hansard) Index

FIGURE 7.1   UK Parliament website: some options from the advanced search page

Parliamentary Publications and Archives (**www.parliament.uk/parliamentary_ publications_and_archives/parliamentary_publications_and_archives. cfm**) This list of publications by the UK Parliament acts as a kind of guide to the materials searchable on the Parliament website, including Hansard and Select Committee Publications.

Official Documents (**www.official-documents.co.uk**)   This includes the full text from the British Government Stationary Office of all command papers, House of Commons papers, and key departmental papers from May 2005 onwards. It also provides a collection of key documents published before that date.

BOPCRIS, the British Official Publications Collaborative Reader Information Service (**www.bopcris.ac.uk**)   A database of British Official Publications between 1688 and 1995. It includes around 40,000 documents, indexed by subject and described in abstracts. It provides the full text of a limited number of documents and information on where to access documents not available online.

UKOP, the official catalogue of UK official publications since 1980 (**www.ukop. co.uk**)   This subscription service includes 450,000 records and is the most comprehensive source of information available on British official publications. It includes the full text of over 30,000 documents.

S Search strategy: searching government sources

Begin a search for government materials by looking for guides produced by the government and by opposition groups to documents on the particular policy you're interested in. These guides will alert you to key collections of documents.

For research on British government policy on Iraq, a quick Google search on **UK government policy Iraq** turns up links to official collections of documents on the topic in the first ten results, including a guide to British government policy produced by the British Foreign and Commonwealth Office. As authoritative and heavily used sources, government sites move to the top of the search results. A key group opposed to US and British policy in Iraq, *IraqWatch*, provides a guide to British government documents on Iraq from a very different perspective. These two guides highlight very different sets of documents but both provide useful starting points.

To find information on a very specific aspect of your topic, you can flexibly combine government sources and keyword search engines. If, for example, you are interested in the way in which the British government has drawn on its experience in Northern Ireland in dealing with security in Iraq, you could search a range of different sources using the query **"Northern Ireland" Basra**. The city of Basra has been the main focus of the British presence in Iraq and provides a very specific search term.

Given that the Foreign and Commonwealth Office (FCO) provides the guide on Iraq policy, you might begin by searching the FCO site. A search on the FCO site for **Basra AND Northern NEAR Ireland** brings back 16 results, including an announcement that a senior policeman from Northern Ireland was sent to Basra to set up policing structures there. It also brings up statements that refer to the importance of experience gained in Northern Ireland.

A similar search through Google on **site:fco.gov.uk Basra "Northern Ireland"** brings back 23 results from the FCO website. The results are not as clearly titled, but they show you the text around your search terms, making it easier to see their relevance to your topic.

You can also limit your search to the IraqWatch collection of British government documents in Google. **site:www.iraqwatch.org/government "Northern Ireland" Basra** brings back four government documents from the IraqWatch site, one of them directly relevant.

A search for **Iraq Basra "Northern Ireland"** on the UK Parliament site that is limited to 'Select Committee Reports' from 2001 onwards brings back more than 30 documents. They include evidence given to committees by government ministers talking about the way in which the military use the exact same techniques in Basra as were used in Northern Ireland.

(Continued)

To search the text of debates in the House of Commons, limit the search to 'Commons Hansard'. A search on **Basra "Northern Ireland"** limited to materials from 2001 onwards brings back more than 20 results, including further remarks by ministers and MPs comparing security tactics in Northern Ireland and Iraq.

A search of the Parliament website through Google does not allow such precise searching: **site:parliament.uk Basra "Northern Ireland"** brings back more than 400 results. The main advantage it has over the Parliament search is the fact that you can see the text around your search terms.

The European Union

All of the European Union member states provide extensive online services of their own, and a list of these national sites is provided on the main EU website (**europa.eu/abc/governments/index_en.htm**). The services dealt with below are concerned primarily with the EU itself rather than with the individual member states. EU institutions, and their complex relationship with the national governments of member states, are clearly explained in the services below, and all of them provide guides to the various online storehouses of EU documentation.

Europa (**europa.eu**)   The official gateway to EU information sources, including guides to EU institutions, databases of EU documentation, materials organized by subject area, and statistical information.

European Sources Online (**www.europeansources.info**)   A commercial online database dealing with the EU and Europe as a whole, it provides introductory guides to European information sources and to EU institutions. Search results are organized by type, identifying them as news items, legislation or reports, for example. It includes official EU information and media reports about the EU.

Intute Social Sciences: EuroStudies (**www.intute.ac.uk/socialsciences/euro studies**)   This section of the Intute Social Sciences Directory includes sources from, and about, the European Union.

European Union Internet Resources (**www.lib.berkeley.edu/doemoff/ govinfo/intl/gov_eu.html**)   This guide from the library at the University of California, Berkeley, provides a concise introduction to the way in which the EU works and a guide to the major collections of documents.

The US government

The US government has the biggest Web presence of any government but it can also lay claim to being one of the most chaotic. There are several different ways of getting access to this information, most of them overlapping but never covering the exact same set of data. It is a world of information in its own right and there are professional searchers who devote their careers to finding their way through this documentation.

A useful guide to the world of US government documentation is the section on the US federal government in *GovInfo* (**www.lib.berkeley.edu/ doemoff/govinfo/federal**), a service of the library at the University of California, Berkeley. It provides brief explanations of the way in which US government institutions work to help you understand the sources you're searching. *Government Resources on the Web* (**www.lib.umich.edu/ libhome/Documents.center/govweb.html**), a guide from the University of Michigan, provides links to information by, and about, the US federal government, US state governments and US local governments.

GPO Access (**www.access.gpo.gov**) This is the online service of the US Government Printing Office, which is legally responsible for printing US government publications. It is the 'official' site for US government publications on the Web. However, the GPO is not responsible for the websites of US government agencies or for much of the output of the US Congress. In addition, some US government agencies publish their own materials and these do not come under the care of the GPO. Thus it provides access to a huge range of US government documents but not, by any means, to all of them.

GPO Access provides several databases, one of the most important of which is the Catalog of US Government Publications (CGP) (**catalog. gpo.gov**). Many of the GPO Access databases are also available elsewhere on the web, sometimes in a form that is easier to search and has more comprehensive coverage. In particular, GPO Access overlaps with the official site for the US Congress, THOMAS.

THOMAS (**thomas.loc.gov**)   Named after Thomas Jefferson, this service of the Library of Congress provides information related to the US Congress, including information about legislation, transcripts of debates and the reports of congressional committees. The committee reports deal with a vast array of subjects and draw on the testimony of experts. They can be a valuable source of information on issues of political debate in the USA.

Fedworld (**www.fedworld.gov**)   This is the official gateway to all US government information online, from official publications through catalogues to government websites. It allows you to search a range of government databases. One of the more useful of these is the NTIS database (National Technical Information Service: **www.ntis.gov**). This is a database of US government reports, or reports funded in part by the US Government, including reports produced by university researchers (Basch, 1998: 184). They are available for free or at little cost. Fedworld is good for identifying useful sites that you can then search individually. You can search US government websites via Fedworld, but you can generally do a more precise and complete search of these sites by going directly to them and using their own search options.

FirstGov (**www.firstgov.gov**) FirstGov is the US government's official web portal, organizing information by organization and topic, and allowing you to jointly search US government websites. It has very useful advanced search facilities. You can limit your search to particular kinds of site and it includes government sites that are not in the **.gov** or **.mil** domains. You can also search FirstGov via the search engine Vivisimo (**Vivisimo.com**) by choosing FirstGov from the drop-down menu there.

Lexis Nexis Congressional (**www.lexisnexis.com**) This is a powerful subscription service that indexes publications of the US Congress, providing access to the full text of many of them. Look for a link from your library or institution.

Google US Government Search (**www.google.com/unclesam**) This service allows you to do a Google search limited to **.mil** and **.gov** websites. There is no advanced search and it misses some government sites that are not in the **.mil** and **.gov** domains. However, it brings back very different results from the FirstGov site, despite the huge overlap in the material they search, and it is useful to use both services in tandem.

Other governments

There is huge variation in the amount and types of material which governments make available on the Web. Many governments have adopted the Internet enthusiastically and put vast amounts of well-organized and valuable information online. This is often aimed primarily at their own citizens as part of a wider aspiration towards provision of more efficient services to citizens (see Hoff et al., 2000). By contrast, some governments, including many of those with repressive political systems, aim their websites primarily at the outside world, rather than at their own citizens. The agencies which are online tend to be those such as tourist boards, industrial development agencies or government information bureau, which have a vested interest in contact with foreign investors, tourists and journalists. *Foreign Government Resources on the Web* (**www.lib.umich.edu/govdocs/ foreign.html**) from the University of Michigan provides links, organized by country, to official government documents and websites and to websites relating to governments around the world.

Archives

Archives used to be quite inaccessible and difficult to use. Because of these difficulties they have been under-utilized as a research resource and many researchers are barely aware that they exist at all. The Internet has facilitated a dramatic opening up of the archives. Collections that could once only be explored and searched by people who went to the archive in person, can now be explored online. In addition, universities and governments are scanning and digitizing large volumes of archive materials that could previously only be viewed by visitors to the archive in question.

Although most national archives are dedicated primarily to preserving records of government activity, they also include a wide range of other materials. Archives commonly include the records of organizations and of private individuals, often people who have been prominent in public life. They also host large quantities of rare materials, of which there may only be a few copies still in existence.

Archives consist of materials created by, or received and accumulated by, a person or organization in the course of the conduct of their affairs, and are preserved because of their continuing value. The term has usually been used to refer to non-current records deposited in an archival institution (Ellis, 1993: 2). They exist in a wide variety of formats and can include paper files, photographs, maps, architectural drawings, films, sound recordings and electronic records.

Understanding archives

To search archives effectively you need to understand how they are organized. Archives are generally organized according to the principles of provenance and original order. To preserve their original intellectual integrity, 'records groups' are formed on the principle of preserving together records generated by the same office, department or other bureaucratic cell or person. The principle of original order involves keeping records in the order in which they were accumulated, as they were created, maintained or used, and not rearranging them according to some latterly imposed subject, numerical, chronological or other order (Ellis, 1993: 11). These principles aim to preserve the context of records and a central purpose of archival catalogues is to provide information about these contexts, to trace the history of the various departments and to explain the way in which those organizations and units ordered their records. Archivists provide this contextual information about their holdings in resources known traditionally as 'finding aids'. These finding aids are now available online in many cases. In addition, many archives provide guides to resources on particular topics and often allow the researcher to search archive catalogues by keyword or by subject. Note that you will generally not be searching the full text of documents, but simply the titles and short descriptions of the files. Some archives provide online help, allowing researchers to contact a specialist in a particular area by email.

Guides to online archives

Ready, net go! (**www.tulane.edu/~1miller/ArchivesResources.html**)   A catalogue of the various guides to archives that are available online.

Repositories of primary sources (**www.uidaho.edu/special-collections/ Other.Repositories.html**)   A simple but useful collection of links to the websites of over 5,000 archives and manuscript repositories around the world, organized geographically.

EAN (European Archival Network) (**www.european-archival.net**)   Intended as the main site for searching for information about European archives, it provides a list of European Archives organized alphabetically and geographically. It gives contact details and website addresses.

The National Archives (US) (archives.gov)

One of the most extensive online archives, the website provides a series of guides on specialized research topics (**archives.gov/publications/finding aids/ guides.html**), including a *Guide to Federal Records in the National Archives of the US.*

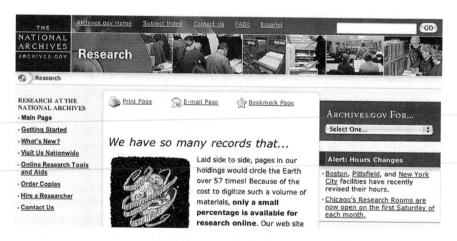

FIGURE 7.2   The US National Archives' home page for researchers

ARC (**archives.gov/research/arc/**) is the main catalogue of the archive's holdings. You can search by keyword, digitized image and location. The advanced search options also allow you to search by organization, person, or topic. When you search ARC you search not only the titles of records but also short descriptions of record groups and sometimes files and individual items. Searches also cover records that have been digitized – a tiny proportion of the total. They include documents and images. You can limit your search to digitized items by selecting the checkbox for 'Descriptions of Archival Materials linked to digital copies'.

AAD: **Access to Archival Databases (aad.archives.gov/aad)** is an archive of databases. It makes around 500 of the 200,000 data files held by the US National Archives available online and allows you to search for information about the other data files.

The National Archives (UK) (www.nationalarchives.gov.uk)

The online catalogue of its holdings includes over 8 million document references with descriptions of the documents and descriptions of the classes in which they are categorized. It provides excellent and detailed research guides on a wide range of topics, from sources for the study of Anglo-Jewish history to treaties. The Archives include the *National Digital Archive of Datasets* (**www.ndad.nationalarchives.gov.uk**), which preserves and provides access to computer datasets from UK government departments and agencies. NDAD provides open access to the catalogues of all its holdings, and free access to open datasets. Another service of the British National Archives, *ARCHON* (**www.nationalarchives.gov.uk/archon/**), is a guide to manuscript sources for British history. From here you can access information on all repositories in the UK, and all those repositories throughout the world that have collections of manuscripts which are noted on the British National Register of Archives.

S   Search strategy: searching an archive

The simplest way to identify relevant archive sources is to look at the key publications in your subject area. Bibliographies and references in these books and articles will give you a good idea of the major archival resources available. These leads can be used, together with the approaches described below, to identify the key sources.

This example illustrates a search for materials in the British National Archives. Every archive is organized differently but the search nonetheless illustrates some of

(Continued)

the general approaches useful in searching archives. In the example, the aim is to identify key collections of records on British policy in Iraq during the 1920s and 1930s, when Britain administered Iraq as a League of Nations 'mandate'.

The first step is to look at the list of the archive's research guides. While none deals specifically with Iraq, a keyword search of the research guides retrieves four guides that mention Iraq. The most useful of these is the guide to sources on the League of Nations. A sub-section in this guide is devoted entirely to the mandates and lists the relevant files on the Iraq mandate, including a range of Colonial Office records: CO 696, CO 730, CO 731, CO 781, CO 782, CO 813. Enter any of these codes in the 'Go to reference' box and you will get a description of the files included under this reference number. The description explains how these particular records fit into the overall administrative structure and briefly describes their contents. It often acts as a pointer to related records that might also be relevant.

You can also search the catalogue by keyword (go to 'Search the archives' and choose 'Search the catalogue'). A general search on **Iraq AND mandate** (limited to the period from 1918 to 1950) returns 20 results. Several of them are from CO 730, which is described as correspondence on Iraq from the 1920s and 1930s. CO 730 includes 178 volumes in total, a massive store of documentation.

Once you have identified the relevant record series, you can limit your searches in the catalogue according to the 'Department or Series code'. Thus, a search on 'Kurds' limited to CO 730 brings back eight files on Kurds in Iraq during the mandate period, all of which are likely to include a wide range of documents.

You can then take a reference number like this and use it to identify books and articles that draw on these archives. This has the dual purpose of getting more information about the contents of these specific files, and pointing users to books that use the archives and are likely to provide pointers to other relevant files on the Iraq mandate.

A search on **"CO 730" Archives Iraq mandate** in Google Scholar returns three results, all of them academic articles about the British mandate in the 1920s and 1930s, all of them using archive sources.

In Google Book Search (**print.google.com**), it returns two recent books, *Inventing Iraq* by Toby Dodge and *The Shi'is of Iraq* by Yitzhak Nakash. Both of them use archive sources extensively and provide useful information on the sources. The same search on Amazon.co.uk only brings up the latter book. In Amazon.com the search brings back no results at first glance, but the link to 'additional results' includes both of the books mentioned in Google Book Search and another two relevant books using archive sources on the Iraq mandate. Between them, these four books provide a store of information about archive sources on the Iraq mandate from researchers who have already spent time in the archives.

Digital archives

Digital archives aim to make the full text of archival materials available online, rather than simply allowing people to search a catalogue of the materials held. As the major archives begin to scan in parts of their collections, the distinction between traditional archive and digital archive has been eroded. Both *OAISTER* (**oaister.umdl.umich.edu/o/oaister/**) and Google Scholar (**scholar.google. com**) search digital archives, although you can't limit your search to them. Below are a number of very specialized digital archives that indicate the kinds of resource that are provided on some topics. If there is a digital archive directly relevant to your subject area, it may well be easier to find it through a good subject guide than through any other method.

Chinese Digital Archive 1966-1976 (**images.anu.edu.au/china.html**)   An archive of photographs, scanned documents and papers focusing on the Chinese Communist Party and the Cultural Revolution. It is maintained by the Australian National University.

The Cornell University Library Witchcraft Collection (**historical.library. cornell.edu/witchcraft/**)   Over many decades Cornell University built up a unique archive of medieval texts on witchcraft. In many cases only a few copies of these books still survive. The full text of more than a 100 of these books has been made freely available in this online collection.

American Memory Project (**memory.loc.gov/ammem/**)   A project of the US Library of Congress that focuses on US history. It includes several million digitized images and texts organized in subject-specific collections.

The Online Archive of California (**www.oac.cdlib.org/**)   The archive draws on the collections of museums, historical societies and archives, and provides over 120,000 images and 50,000 pages of documents, letters and oral histories.

Conflict Archive on the Internet: CAIN (**cain.ulst.ac.uk**)   This project of the University of Ulster has archived a huge collection of materials related to violent conflict in Northern Ireland. Through agreement with authors, publishers, organizations and members of the public, it has scanned in pamphlets, posters, leaflets and large private collections of photographs. It has also made the text of a wide range of published journal articles and book chapters, some of them out of print, available free of charge through arrangements with individual authors and publishers.

Statistics

Many researchers will never need to go beyond the statistics used in books and academic articles. Even those that do will find most of what they need in the reports by statistical agencies that summarize statistics on various topics. If you do need to explore the statistics in more detail, it's important to know more or less exactly what you're looking for before you start dealing with the raw data.

Statistical bodies provide statistics in a number of different forms. For many researchers it will be more than enough to read the reports analysing the data, the simplest form in which it is available. You can also get access to statistical tables online, the kinds of table which used to be contained in a government census publication, listing numbers according to age or birthplace or nationality, for example. You can print them out and look at them. They're useful in their own right but they're static. You can't manipulate the data. You can't play around with it and ask for different results.

Increasingly, statistics providers allow you to manipulate and analyse their data on their websites. You can use pull-down menus and query boxes on the websites to crunch the numbers yourself and produce tables customized to your own research needs. This is less flexible than having the data yourself, but it means you have an easy-to-use interface and you don't need to learn how to use a complex piece of statistical software.

Some statistics providers now make the raw statistical data available as data files which you can download to your own computer. You can then open them up on a piece of statistical software such as SPSS and perform very sophisticated analyses of the statistics. This is really only for those with a reasonably advanced knowledge of how to use the statistics. In many cases you can only get access to data files if you are a registered user or if you pay for them.

Collecting data

New methods for gathering original data online through online surveys, questionnaires and focus groups, online ethnography, web sphere analysis and a range of other methods have been developed in recent years. Online research methods is a major topic in its own right so it is not dealt with in detail here. Rather, see books and articles such as Jones (1998); Kaye and Johnson (1999); Kollock and Smith (1999); Hine (2000, 2005); Mann and Stewart (2000); Nesbary (2000); and Best and Krueger (2004).

Search strategy: searching for statistics

Start by searching for academic articles, reports and studies on your topic that use statistical sources. This is one of the simplest ways to identify relevant statistical sources. To identify recent statistics on European attitudes to immigration, for example, search Google Scholar for **attitudes immigration Europe statistics**. Limit the search to articles published after 2002 in the advanced search to exclude earlier articles that use out-of-date statistics.

Among the first few results is an article that draws on the Eurobarometer surveys to discuss attitudes to immigration. It's a simple matter to get to the Eurobarometer home page (**europa.eu.int/comm/public_opinion/index_en.htm**) from any search engine. Other results from the initial Google search refer to the 2003 European Social Survey (**www.europeansocialsurvey.org**) and the British Social Attitudes Survey. All of these surveys have generated reports and publications that analyse the data they provide on attitudes to immigration.

You can use the names of any of these surveys, combined with key terms on the topic, to identify further academic work and public debate that refers to these surveys. Thus a Google Scholar search on **"British Social Attitudes" immigration** turns up over 250 sources, many of which draw on the survey for discussions of attitudes to immigration. In Amazon.com, the same search turns up the published report of the 19th British Social Attitudes Survey, allowing you to search inside the book for references to immigration in the report. In Google Book Search, it brings up 29 books, including the 21st report of the survey and several other directly relevant books. In Google it turns up over 10,000 results, including many news sources summarizing some of the key conclusions.

You can use the text of survey questions to make your search even more specific. One key question in the Eurobarometer survey uses the distinctive phrase "the presence of foreigners", which can be used as a specialized search term to identify other articles that refer to this particular question.

Thus a Google search on **"the presence of foreigners" Eurobarometer** turns up 120 results, many of them concerned directly with European attitudes to immigration. Among these results are several reports from Europa, the central European site that hosts Eurobarometer.

Guides to statistical sources
WebStat (**www.linkkitalo.fi/webstaten**) This organizes and describes around 3,000 statistical sources available online, organized by theme and searchable by keyword. It is a service of the Library of Statistics Finland.

Offstats (**www.library.auckland.ac.nz/subjects/stats/offstats**)   This links to official statistical resources worldwide, organized geographically and by topic. A service of the University of Auckland library.

Statistical Resources on the Web (**www.lib.umich.edu/libhome/documents. center/stats.html**)   This service, from the University of Michigan, organizes statistical resources by broad subject categories, including several social science categories such as sociology, economics and politics.

UK Statistics

National Statistics (**www.statistics.gov.uk**) is the Official UK statistics website, organizing material by subject areas such as migration, education and economy. The site provides information about newly released datasets.

European Union statistics

The European Union's statistical role is focused on coordinating and harmonizing statistical work by the official statistics bodies in its member states. These national statistics offices are listed in the guides mentioned above. *Eurostat* (**www.eu.int/comm/eurostat/**), the European Union's Statistical Information Service, takes the lead role in this and produces statistical reports based on data from the various member states. The European Union does gather its own data in some areas. For example, *Eurobarometer* (**europa.eu.int/comm/public_opinion/standard_en.htm**), the Public Opinion Analysis sector of the European Commission, carries out regular surveys of public opinion across the EU, dealing with contemporary political issues. It provides reports summarizing the results.

United States statistics

FirstGov provides a 'Data and Statistics – General Reference Resources' section that provides a useful guide to US government data and statistical resources (**www.firstgov.gov/Topics/Reference_Shelf/Data.shtml**). One of the central sources of statistical data on the USA is the US Census Bureau (**www.census.gov**). *FedStats* (**www.fedstats.gov**) provides a guide to the statistical data produced by over 100 US federal government agencies, organized by subject and geographically. It provides links to statistical publications and reports, and you can search individual agencies or search them jointly.

For advanced research, the subscription service *LexisNexis Statistical* provides access to statistical sources from over 200 US federal agencies, 100 international intergovernmental organizations and hundreds of other sources. Look for a link from your library's web pages.

International statistics

The UN Statistics Division (**www.un.org/Depts/unsd**) provides a range of statistical databases drawing together data from national statistical agencies around the world on topics such as housing, population and gender. They also provide a number of subscription databases.

SourceOECD (**www.sourceoecd.org**), the Organization for Economic Cooperation and Development's Online Library, includes a large number of international statistical databases on employment, health, education, international migration and trade.

Data archives

Data archives hold and preserve datasets gathered by a wide variety of organizations and research projects. In many cases they allow users to download the full datasets to analyse them on their own computers. Data files may exist in a definitive version and be generated by a project or business function with a finite timespan, or a data file may be dynamic, constantly evolving, generated by a project or business function with no finite timescale (Feeney, 1999: 10).

ICPSR: The Inter-university Consortium for Political and Social Research (**www.icpsr.umich.edu**) ICPSR provides access to the world's largest archive of computerized social science data. Access to the datasets is restricted to those affiliated to member colleges and universities. Everybody can get access to abstracts and other documentation related to many of the datasets. You can search for datasets by subject, title and keyword.

CESSDA: Council for European Social Science Data Archives (**www.nsd. uib.no/cessda/**) Cessda allows you to simultaneously search the catalogues of data archives in several countries, mostly in Europe but also including the ICPSR in the USA. It also provides links to these catalogues.

The UK Data Archive (**www.data-archive.ac.uk**) An extensive collection of datasets and related documentation in the social sciences and humanities. The collection consists mainly of datasets that were gathered in the course of publicly funded research projects in the UK. Many of these are surveys carried out by government agencies or public bodies. You can search by subject and keyword. It also provides access for academic researchers in the UK to some of the ICPSR datasets and to European-based data archives. A tutorial (**tramss.data-archive.ac.uk/index.asp**) teaches you how to analyse the data in the UK data archive, and how to download datasets and even the relevant software, although it does require some basic understanding of statistical analysis.

Exercises

Exercise 1: Government information

Identify a government likely to have produced materials relevant to your research. Search for guides to government documents on your research topic produced by this government and by a group opposed to this government's policy in that area.

Identify the government department or unit most directly concerned with your topic.

Search its website to identify documents or collections of documents relevant to your research.

Search the same website using the same search terms via two of the following services:

- Google
- Yahoo
- MSNSearch

Briefly describe the differences between the results of these different searches.

Search the proceedings of the relevant legislature/parliament/assembly using very specific keywords related to your topic.

Search the reports of legislative/parliamentary committees using the same keywords.

Briefly describe the results.

How useful were these searches?

Briefly describe the search process as a whole, the most productive part of the search, the difficulties you encountered, and any advice you would give to someone else embarking on a similar search.

Exercise 2: Searching archives

Find an academic article or book relevant to your research that uses archive sources. Use that article or book to identify an archive that is likely to hold materials relevant to your research, and to identify records that might be relevant.

Search for a research guide at that archive that deals with your subject area and use it to identify key records.

Identify other relevant records by searching the archive using broad search terms related to your topic.

Identify further relevant records by searching the archive using very specific terms related to your topic.

Describe the overlap and the differences between the results produced by these four different search methods.

Go to the descriptions of several of the most promising-looking records you have identified through these searches. Pick out two or three record series' or files that are most likely to be of use to you.

Use the reference codes for these files, the term 'archives', and a key term associated with your topic area to search in the following sources for publications that use these archives. If the code for an individual file is too specific to retrieve results, use the code for the record series that file belongs to, in order to make the search broader.

- Google Scholar
- Amazon.com
- Amazon.co.uk
- Google Books

Describe the results. How useful are they?

Carry out the same search in two of the search engines below:

- MSN Search
- Yahoo
- Google

Describe and compare the results from the two services. How useful are they?

Briefly describe the search process as a whole, the most productive part of the search, the difficulties you encountered, and any advice you would give to someone else embarking on a similar search.

Exercise 3: Statistics

Search for academic articles and books relevant to your research that use statistical data. Use these publications to identify a statistical source relevant to your research.

Use the names of this source, combined with one or two key terms on your topic, to identify further academic work and reports that refer to this source. Search in the following services:

- Google Scholar
- Amazon.com
- Amazon.co.uk
- Google Books

Find the web pages for the statistical source and identify the relevant reports on your topic (search Google, Yahoo or MSNSearch for the name of the survey or agency and, if necessary, the topic).

(Continued)

Using the name of the source and a distinctive phrase from one of the survey questions that relates directly to your topic, search for sources that make direct reference to this question. Search in the following services:

- Google Scholar
- Amazon.com
- Amazon.co.uk
- Google Books

Briefly describe the results. How useful are they?

Do the same search in at least two of these services:

- Google
- Yahoo
- MSNSearch

Describe and compare the results from the two services. How useful are they?

Briefly describe the search process as a whole, the most productive part of the search, the difficulties you encountered, and any advice you would give to someone else embarking on a similar search.

8
Evaluation and citation

Introduction

Lies and propaganda have always been with us. They don't originate with the Internet and they're not confined to the Internet. However, the Internet does mean that academic researchers and students are less insulated from highly problematic sources than they used to be (see Mintz, 2002). A central, if largely invisible, function of publishers and libraries is to exclude, screening out a huge range of materials in the process of selecting resources for publication or purchase. This ongoing work of exclusion shielded researchers and students from a huge proportion of the information circulating in the world. Now that we have access to a much wider range of sources, we have to develop new skills to evaluate them. It is necessary to become much more sensitive to the wide range of indicators that provide an indication of the character and reliability of an online source. The new information environment necessitates a much more actively critical approach to the sources we use.

In judging information sources, we draw unconsciously on a wide range of visual and contextual cues. We are more inclined to rely on a footnoted book from a university press located in a university library than on a scribbled note written on the back of a stained beer-mat in a bar. The academic book might be a discredited work, subsequently shown to be riddled with errors. The beer-mat note might have been written by one of the foremost experts in the field, but their appearance and location will play a powerful role in determining our judgement of them.

The visual and contextual clues that help us to make a judgement on the reliability of a source are not completely absent online but they are far less obvious. The online equivalents of the beer-mat note and the academic book are much closer in appearance than their offline counterparts.

Evaluating online sources requires developing your awareness of a range of much subtler indications of a source's reliability. This is not to suggest that all academic sources are reliable and unbiased, or to imply that non-academic sources as a whole are not. Like their offline counterparts, the online equivalent of the beer-mat may well be a more useful and relevant source to you than the online equivalent of the academic book.

Because it can be so much more difficult to evaluate the reliability of online sources and because they are so much less controlled than the resources available in a library, many in academia express extreme scepticism of the value of any online source. There is a tendency to seek to resolve the issues around evaluation and quality by excluding Internet sources. Much of this scepticism is well founded, but the response to these challenges is not to turn away from online sources. Instead, it is important to develop critical information literacy, a new set of skills to help us to develop a better understanding of the materials we are looking at, to allow us to evaluate authority and credibility and to understand the context in which materials have been produced.

Classification

A useful starting point for evaluating online sources is to begin with a rough classification of the materials you are dealing with. Classifying involves putting a document in a necessarily crude category in order to be able to assess it according to the standards appropriate to that category. When you've decided a document is a news document, you won't be disappointed that it's not footnoted. You won't expect an advocacy document to be neutral. Conversely, when an academic document clearly falls short of the standards of proof that you expect of such materials, you have a right to be particularly sceptical of its conclusions. The categories given here are necessarily crude and you will find that a lot of web pages are difficult to fit into one category or another. The guidelines below are not intended as a set of rigid instructions to be followed mechanically, but as a series of questions that can usefully be asked about any online materials. Doing this is valuable in itself, allowing you to develop a better understanding of the nature of the source.

Advocacy

Advocacy groups such as political parties, non-governmental organizations or pressure groups advocate a particular cause or viewpoint. They weigh up competing arguments as they develop these positions but that process of weighing up is not their prime concern. The advancement of a particular point of view is their core purpose.

Some advocacy groups systematically and deliberately distort and exaggerate facts in pursuit of their aims. On the other hand, many advocacy groups produce work of extremely high quality. The work of groups such as the *Minority Rights Group* (**www.minorityrights.org**) and *Amnesty International* (**www.amnesty.org**) draws on academic standards while also seeking to have a direct political impact. They are valuable academic resources and we need to be careful not to approach all advocacy documents with unduly high levels of scepticism.

Generally you will recognize an advocacy document because it will be clearly marked with the name of the group that produced it. If not, the name of the group should be there on the site home page. Although many advocacy groups use the **.org** domain, not all such groups use the domain so the URL does not provide a reliable guide, although many try to avoid the **.com** domain. Be aware that some advocacy groups try to give their arguments more credibility by making themselves sound like academic organizations with titles like the 'Centre for research on ...' or the 'Institute for the study of ...'.

It can be difficult to distinguish an advocacy document from a personal page since so many individuals put up pages advocating particular views. An individual may well set up an organization of which he or she is the founder, president and sole member. In the sense in which I use the term, such a one-person show should not be considered an advocacy group and their output on the Web should be treated as personal pages rather than advocacy documents. They should be treated with the especially high levels of caution appropriate for such pages.

Advocacy documents are problematic mainly because they often only give one side of a story. There is one simple and obvious way to correct this imbalance – get the other side of the story. If an advocacy group is on the web, it's likely their opponents are also online.

Academia

Academic documents undergo some sort of quality control, whether it be the examination process a thesis or dissertation goes through, the peer review which journal articles are subject to, or the editorial process academic books go through. Academic documents are accorded a certain degree of authority because of the experience of authors, reflected in their academic qualifications and their other publications. This isn't to say that all academic work is perfect, merely that it has gone through a set of procedures that provide at least some sort of quality control.

Academia attracts a certain amount of respect, as a source of unbiased research. As a result, certain advocacy groups, businesses and news sources try to make their documents look like academic documents. Several countries have domains which are reserved for academic institutions, **edu** in the

USA, **ac.uk** in Britain, **ac.jp** in Japan, **edu.au** in Australia, for example. In other countries the universities are easily recognized by their web addresses. In Germany, **www.uni-oldenburg.de** is Oldenburg University, **www.uni-heidelberg.de** is Heidelberg University and so on.

Not all documents on university servers are academic documents. The mountains of materials that universities provide about themselves are best classified as 'official' documents (see below). Many universities also allow students to create websites on the university's web server. These are personal pages (see below), and in some cases advocacy documents, and should be treated as such.

There are now large numbers of academic draft papers and works in progress on the web. Although these are clearly academic documents, you cannot treat them like published articles. In many cases authors stipulate that you should not quote from or cite these articles without direct permission from the author. You can read them and print them, but you can only cite them after you go to the trouble of contacting the author, assuming your own supervisor is happy for you to use materials which haven't taken final form.

Official documents

Official documents are those produced by public institutions, and by government and international agencies. They include documents from the smallest local council or fire department up to national bodies such as government departments and agencies. They include documents from international organizations, from the UN and OPEC to NATO and the OSCE.

Many governments have their own domain (**gov** in the USA, **gov.uk** in Britain, **gov.jp** in Japan) or their government affiliation is often clear from their URL. In Germany and in Denmark, for example, government ministries have web addresses that include abbreviations of the ministries' titles. The German Environment Ministry, the BMU, is **www.bmu.de**, while the URL for the Irish government is **www.irlgov.ie**. Many US states have their own domains. Thus **ca.gov** is the domain for the California state government. Some US states have domains that do not come under the overall **gov** domain, such as New York State, whose domain is **state.ny.us**. Government domains in most cases only cover central government. Local and regional bodies often make their own arrangements and it is not as straightforward to identify them by their URLs. Political considerations do of course influence official documents, and in certain cases they shade over into clear advocacy of particular positions.

The boundary between official and news sources can be unclear. Many countries have official news agencies connected to government, such as Xinhua in China. Despite being government agencies, their prime function is to provide news. Apart from this, many governments issue press releases and print publications to promote the government currently in power. These are not news services but they sometimes look like they are, particularly on the web where it's easy to put together a collection of government statements and call them a news bulletin or news update.

News

Traditional news sources such as wire services, newspapers, TV and radio news programmes, and magazines are being joined by new media sources such as news blogs and alternative online news sources such as Indymedia (**www.indymedia.org**). The line between government and advocacy groups and news sources can be quite unclear at times. News sources do tend to be informed by a particular political viewpoint. This is reflected in the way they cover news stories, in the stories they choose to cover, in the aspects of a story they emphasize and in the editorial positions they take. In many cases news sources have more direct political affiliations. If you are using an unfamiliar news source, you need to be aware that many news sources across the world are directly linked to political parties or governments, and their approach to the news can be even more partisan than you would usually expect from a news source. Many new media sources are much more openly partisan in their coverage than traditional media.

Most online newspapers still follow the basic layout of the print version – a front page with short summaries of stories that appear inside – so that you recognize them as news sources immediately from their familiar layout. Likewise, the websites of TV news services are clearly identified. The wire services provide news stories to huge numbers of other Web services but they always clearly stamp their name on the individual news stories. These are news documents no matter what kind of site they appear on.

As with academia, the news media has a reasonably high level of credibility. Some advocacy groups imitate the style, layout and terminology of news documents in an attempt to increase their credibility.

News sources, like academia, aspire to the pursuit of truth and the ideal of objectivity. Unlike academia, news sources set lower formal standards of proof and referencing of sources. They are not footnoted. They can and do give the opinions of individuals as though they represent the opinions of an entire group. Standards vary from one news organization to another, and those papers that attempt to be papers of record, recording all significant events with the intention of acting as a source for researchers in the future, are invaluable as research sources. Many news sources have only the barest consideration for the ideals of objectivity and put considerably more weight on another core purpose of news-gathering: the selling of news as a product.

Personal pages

The recent expansion of services such as Myspace and Bebo has made it a simple matter for anyone with Internet access to set up their own web page and blog. Millions of children, teenagers and adults have web pages that are primarily concerned with their private lives. Many people use their web pages to express their personal opinions on matters of public debate, but few of them expect that others will rely on these private pages as authoritative sources of information. The informal tone and presentation mark these contributions to public debate as essentially private expressions of opinion.

There are a number of crude measures for assessing the value and reliability of a personal page. As the product of a single individual, its reliability will depend on this individual alone. You can look for indicators of how much trust to place in them. Consider what their qualifications to write on the subject are. These qualifications can range from academic degrees to direct personal experience to previous publications on the topic. Finally, evaluate them for accuracy and objectivity, as outlined below.

Business/marketing pages

These are pages set up by commercial companies with the core purpose of selling a product and promoting the company. While they may provide useful information about the company, this information is there to promote the company and its products. When using such pages you have to be constantly aware of this fact and of the very important consequences it has for the reliability of the information provided. Be aware that businesses do sometimes try to present their materials as 'news' or 'research' to give it more credibility.

The **.com** domain was created for businesses and is used by businesses worldwide. In addition, many countries outside the USA have their own commercial domains, such as **.co.uk** in the UK. Just because a site has a **.com** address doesn't automatically make it a business/marketing site, however. Many news organizations, advocacy groups and private individuals use the **.com** domain.

Evaluation

One of the main purposes of evaluating online materials is to judge how trustworthy or reliable a source they are. A second purpose is to identify the sort of information which is immediately obvious in print publications – information about the publisher and author. This information is essential if you are to cite online materials accurately. What follows is a series of checklists to help you assess authority, accuracy, objectivity, currency and quality.

It draws heavily on the categories used by Alexander and Tate (1999), elaborating on and reorganizing the categories a little. Don't apply these evaluation criteria too rigidly. Sometimes the most reliable and authoritative of web pages do not include the basic information mentioned in these checklists. Governments, for example, often neglect to stamp their authority clearly on many documents. They often don't bother with footnoting, copyright statements or contact details. It illustrates the fact that those with most authority often feel the least need to proclaim it.

Authority

The author, the organization or institution he or she is associated with and the publisher of the work are the main sources of authority for print publications, in varying degree. Details for each of these are usually provided in print publications.

On a web page, author, organization and publisher can easily be combined in the one person and they can often be quite difficult to identify. There are several questions one can ask.

1. Is it clear who is responsible for the document?

That may be an individual author, an organization or the website owners or publishers. If you can't find this information on the document you're looking at, check if it's available on the front page for that site. The author of a website or blog may simply have copied and pasted information from somewhere else. He or she may well have altered it and given incorrect information about it. In this case you need to track down the original.

2. Is there any information about the person or organization responsible for the page?

Is there any information that would help you to make a judgement about how reliable the author is? In print publications the very fact that a book has been published by a well-established publisher with a good reputation, or has been written by someone with a qualification in the subject they're writing on, lends it a certain credibility. If you're unsure of the quality of the page, you might look to see if any information has been provided about the author or the organization.

3. Is there a copyright statement?

In the absence of a clear statement of who the author is, a copyright statement provides an alternative indication of who is responsible for the document. Don't be too upset if you don't find a copyright statement. Many people don't bother because materials are automatically copyrighted to their author regardless of whether they include a copyright statement or not.

4. Does it have a print counterpart that reinforces its authority?

Print documents in general are regarded as more reliable than web documents. If a web document also has a print version, that is, if it has appeared in a print publication such as a book, journal or newspaper, it reinforces its authority.

Accuracy

There are several questions users can ask to assure themselves of the accuracy of sources.

1. Are sources clearly listed so they can be verified?

This is a fundamental requirement of academic literature, in the form of footnotes and bibliographies. Although you can't expect non-academic documents to follow academic footnoting conventions, you can usefully pose this question of all documents. You can use it as a measure of the quality and reliability of advocacy documents in particular.

2. Is there an editorial input?

An editor provides an extra layer of quality control which should lead to increased accuracy. Most print publications have been through an editorial process.

3. Is spelling and grammar correct?

You should be careful not to place too much weight on spelling and grammar. Minor errors creep into virtually every publication. However, poor spelling and grammar can indicate a certain carelessness that might affect the document in other ways. If an author has got his or her spelling wrong, then maybe they've got some of the facts wrong too.

Objectivity

It is unrealistic to expect anyone writing on the human and the social world in which all of us are immersed to be detached and objective about their subject. In recent years many in academia have argued against the ideals of detached objectivity on the grounds that it often serves to mask prejudice and bias in the research community. The aspiration to objectivity, however impossible it may be to achieve, is a traditional value of academic research. In practical terms it means that you should not allow your personal preferences to interfere with your research, that you should not distort evidence, that you should not make wild claims based on weak evidence and not deliberately omit evidence. You are entitled to expect academic documents to make more of an attempt at objectivity than, for example, advocacy documents. But just because a document doesn't attempt to be objective doesn't render it worthless. The questions below can usefully be applied to a wide range of documents.

1. Are biases and affiliations clearly stated?
You can expect that an advocacy document will advocate a particular position. The real problem arises when they do not make this clear.

2. Is advertising clearly differentiated from information?
Advertisers often try to present ads in the form of newspaper articles or research findings to give them more credibility. This is deliberately misleading and seriously undermines the credibility of a document.

Currency

Currency means checking the date when the document was produced or last updated to see how up to date it is. If you want to know about the current state of the Nicaraguan economy, for example, it's very important that the documents you're relying on should be as up to date as possible.

In many cases it's not important to the researcher that a document is current. However, it's still important to identify the date when a document was produced. It identifies the historical context for the document. Thus, it's important to know whether a document dealing with the Second World War was produced in the midst of the war, shortly after it or many years later. The period in which it was produced will have a powerful influence on the document, and knowing the date will help you to understand the document. Here are some questions to be aware of.

1. If the document has a print counterpart, is there a date of publication for that?
If there is a print counterpart, and the web version is an unaltered copy of the print version, then the date of the print publication is the only significant date. It's generally irrelevant when it was put on the Web or when you viewed it.

2. Are there dates for when the document was first produced or first put on the Web?
For a document with no print counterpart, these are two different ways of determining when a web document was first 'published'.

3. Are there dates for when the document was last updated or revised?
For those documents that are regularly updated it's important to indicate which version you are referring to. The date when it was last updated also indicates how current and up to date the document is. Note that most

web authors don't bother to 'constantly update' the documents they put on the Web.

Evaluating email messages

It can be tricky to assess the reliability of email messages as research sources. Personal messages stand on their own merits. You place as much reliability on them as you would on the person who sent them. The same applies to messages sent via email distribution lists by organizations and institutions. You trust them as much as you trust the sender.

Things become more difficult when you're dealing with forwarded messages. People often forward by email news stories or other items they've gleaned from the web. In some cases people edit or alter the stories, for legitimate reasons, highlighting the section they want to bring to your attention. In many cases, though, people edit to make news reports appear more favourable to their argument or political position. Be very careful of quoting from an item that has been forwarded to you in the body of an email message (if it's an attachment it's a little less likely to have been altered). You need to check the original and cite the original wherever possible.

T   The sunscreen speech and the dangers of relying on email messages

---

In July or August 1997 someone sent an email message that included the text of a short speech which began with the words: 'Wear sunscreen. If I could offer you only one tip for the future, sunscreen would be it.' They described it as a speech that the science-fiction author Kurt Vonnegut had given at a commencement ceremony at the Massachusetts Institute of Technology (MIT) in Boston. It was a clever speech and a lot of people forwarded it on to friends via email. People put copies of it on websites, attributing authorship to Vonnegut. It came to the attention of filmmaker Baz Luhrman (*Romeo and Juliet, Strictly Ballroom, Moulin Rouge*), who decided to record a song using the text of the speech. When he started searching the Internet for contact details for Vonnegut, so that he could buy the rights to the words, he came across web pages that discussed the speech. It turned out that Kurt Vonnegut had never made such a speech, had never in fact spoken at an MIT commencement ceremony. Columnist Mary Schmich had written the original piece as a column in the *Chicago Tribune* in June 1997. Why the person who first included it in an email message described it as a speech by Vonnegut is a mystery, but as a result thousands of people believed Vonnegut had said it. The moral of the story? Be careful of anything that has been forwarded to you by email. Do your best to find the original source of the information.

Source: Ahrens (1999)

Citation

The central purposes of citation are to acknowledge your sources, to provide information about the sources that help us to understand the context in which they were produced (such as date, publisher and author), and to make it possible for the reader to track down and consult the original sources. When you're citing online sources you need to bear in mind these core purposes. A URL on its own does not acknowledge the author, does not provide much information about the source and is often not sufficient to guide a reader back to the original source. Authors change their web pages. They move them to new URLs. They delete them.

No matter how carefully you cite Internet sources you can never guarantee that your reader will be able to access those sources. You can insure yourself against the disappearance of your sources by systematically saving and/or printing copies of all of the online sources you plan to cite. All of the major web browsers allow you to save web pages. If you want to make sure you have archived all of the complex elements of a site, Adobe Acrobat and Internet Explorer have sophisticated web page archiving capacities. There are also many specialized Web archiving software packages, including DeepVacuum, MM3-WebAssistant, WebHTTrack, WebReaper, wget and WinHTTrack. The online bookmarking site FURL (**furl.net**) provides another way to archive sites you intend to refer to.

Make sure the date and URL are included on printouts, changing the print preferences in your Web browser if necessary. If a source disappears or changes and you haven't saved it, you can always try searching the Internet Archive (**www.archive.org**) for a copy. This advice does not apply to online documents that have print counterparts, such as books, articles or reports. You don't need to save or print them. They are not likely to disappear or be altered in the same way that web pages are.

If an item that you find online has a print counterpart, just cite the print version according to normal citation guidelines. This applies in particular to books, academic journals, and newspaper and magazine articles. The fact that you access these sources online is irrelevant. Some of the most authoritative citation guidelines recommend that you cite the database in which you found an academic article or book, the full URL and the date you accessed it. This is excessive and makes citations unnecessarily long. It's like asking you to identify the library shelf you found a book on and to describe the weather at the time. It is not necessary to guide the reader to the original source and it does not add to our understanding of the item. Unfortunately, if your institution, department or supervisor insists that you follow these guidelines to the letter, you will have no choice but to include this redundant information. If you are citing an article from a journal with no print counterpart, you should provide the URL, indicating that this is a purely online source.

If you can't properly cite the materials you use, if you can't mark out a path that will allow the reader to find the original sources you're referring to, they'll be entitled to be sceptical of those sources. The very fact that you will be able to assess and cite web documents according to rigorous academic standards is the most powerful argument you can have against the scepticism of those who are suspicious of any Internet-based source.

Emerging citation standards

In recent years some of the main authorities responsible for setting standards for the citation of print documents have laid down guidelines for Internet citation. The American Psychological Association (APA) provides well-developed guidelines on 'electronic references' (**www.apastyle.org/elecref.html**), while the Modern Languages Association provides an online summary of the MLA guidelines that cover online sources (**www.mla.org/publications/style/style_ faq/style_faq4**). *The Columbia Guide to Online Style* (Walker and Taylor, 1998) also provides a basic introduction to Internet citation online (**www.columbia.edu/cu/cup/cgos/idx_basic.html**). To find a wide variety of advice sheets on citation, search any search engine for '**citation guidelines**' and the name of the style you wish to use.

The examples of citation given below use the Harvard referencing system, also known as the author–date system. It is the most widely used system in the social and physical sciences. It is used here to illustrate the main elements needed in the citation of online sources rather than to lay down a single standard. These guidelines provide useful advice no matter what citation style you use. Make sure that the citation style you use conforms to the guidelines laid down by your institution, department or supervisor.

Citation elements

To cite a web page or a blog post you need to use most of the elements of a book citation, adapted to suit the Internet. You also need to identify the wider context in which the online item is located, as you have to do with a print journal article. In the case of an academic article, that context is the journal it appeared in. On the web that wider context is the website a document belongs to, or the blog an entry was made in. In the case of email messages and posts to discussion groups, that wider context is the email list a message belongs to (where applicable) or the group a message was posted to. The other additional element in an Internet citation is the URL. It can be particularly difficult to deal with dates in citing online materials and this issue is dealt with in more detail below.

Table 8.1 compares the different elements used in citing print sources, such as books and articles, and those used in citing online sources.

TABLE 8.1   Citation elements for online and offline sources

Citation elements	Book	Article	Web page	Blog entry	Email/Post to a group
Author	X	X	X	X	X
Year	X	X	X	X	X
Title	X	X (of the article)	X (of the page)	X (of the entry)	X (the subject header or discussion title)
Journal		X			
Site			X (the website it belongs to)	X (the name of the blog)	X (the discussion group or email list)
Volume		X			
Issue		X			
Pages		X			
Place	X				
Publisher	X				
URL			X	X	X (for a group)
Date			X (date viewed/ accessed. Only if essential: see below)	X (the date the entry was posted)	X (the date the email was sent or the post was posted)

Author

Authors of blog posts, email messages and discussion group posts are clearly identified, even if that identity is often a nickname or pseudonym. The authors of web pages can be more difficult to identify. If the author of a web page is not clearly identified on the document, check the home page of the site to see if the author is identified there. If the document is produced by an organization, whether that be a government, an advocacy group or a business firm, it may well be that the organization itself is the author. You can assume this if no author is specified. In the case of news items, journalists are often not given a by-line, that is, their name does not appear with the article. In that case, you do not need to give an author name. The news agency or publication is effectively the author and they will appear in the citation in any case.

Title

All web documents have a 'title' field the author can fill in. This is what appears in the bar at the very top of your browser. Many authors don't fill it in and many who do put a different title here from the one visible on the page itself. If the two are different, you should probably use the title which is visible on the page. If it looks like the title, it probably is the title.

Site

When you cite a published journal article, you always include the name of the journal in which it was published. It is equally important in web citation that you cite the website a document belongs to, or the blog a message was posted to. It explains the wider context in which the item is located. Refer back to Chapter 4 for a detailed explanation of what constitutes a site if you have difficulty in identifying the site.

URL

There are a few complications around citing URLs. Many services create pages 'on-the-fly', that is, the page is created for you in response to your request. For example, a news service with a huge archive of news stories may offer you the option of clicking on stories on crime. The page it retrieves is not a pre-existing web page which would have its own URL. Rather, it is the result of a search query. The URL will reflect this, being very long, full of numbers and making no sense. In this case, it is often impractical and of little use to cite the URL and it's more important to note details of author, title and site.

Frames can cause major problems for web citation by obscuring the URLs of the pages you are looking at. If you keep seeing the same URL in the bar at the top of the browser as you move to different pages, then this is the URL of the frame itself, not the pages you're looking at. To see the URL, print out the document (ensuring that the print preferences are set to include the URL) or use 'back' to return to the previous page and scan over the link to see the URL. To bookmark an individual page within a framed site so you can check the URL of the bookmark, right-click on the page itself and choose 'add bookmark'.

Given that the vast majority of URLs begin with **http://**, you can omit that part of the URL in your citations. None of the major search engines require you to enter **http://** when you enter the URL and it is therefore unnecessary in directing people back to the source.

Date

For many online documents only one date is needed for a citation, the date when the document was first written or the closest equivalent, such as the date it was first put on the web. A huge proportion of documents are neither changed nor updated after they go on to a website and the date when you viewed these pages is irrelevant. If a document is subject to change, you need to include the date when it was last updated, if it is provided on the page. This indicates the version of the document that you saw. You are not guaranteeing that the document will look the same after the next update.

The third type of date is only relevant to undated documents or to documents that change but do not provide a 'last updated' date, through neglect or carelessness. In this case, and in this case only, you should put down the date on which you viewed it. In the examples below, the term 'accessed' is used. The APA citation guidelines suggest the word 'retrieved'. Whichever word you choose, be sure to use it consistently. This date indicates that you are citing the document as it appeared on the day you viewed it. You are not guaranteeing that it will look the same after that date. When a document is undated, use 'n.d.' for the year of publication, as in the first example below.

The examples below illustrate four different forms that the citation of a web page might take, depending on the information it provides about dates and on whether it is subject to updating. It's a document called 'Small victories in the kitchen' by an imaginary author, Anna Lee, one of several documents by the author on a site called *Rat Wars*.

No information about dates is provided
Lee, Anna (n.d.) 'Small victories in the kitchen', *Rat Wars* <www.anysite.com/members/~annalee/ratwars/kitchen.html> Accessed: 12 March 2007.

A date when it was first written or first put on the Web is provided – it is clear that the document has not been updated since and is unlikely to be updated
Lee, Anna (2005) 'Small victories in the kitchen', *Rat Wars* <www.anysite.com/members/~annalee/ratwars/kitchen.html>.

A date when it was first written or first put on the Web is provided – it has been updated since and the date of last updating is provided
Lee, Anna (2005) 'Small victories in the kitchen', *Rat Wars* <www.anysite.com/members/~annalee/ratwars/kitchen.html> Updated: 10 September 2007.

A date when it was first written or first put on the Web is provided – it appears to have been updated since but the date of last updating is not provided
Lee, Anna (2005) 'Small victories in the kitchen', *Rat Wars* <www.anysite.com/members/~annalee/ratwars/kitchen.html> Accessed: 12 March 2007.

There will be times when you need to cite an entire website or blog, rather than a single post or web page, in the same way you might cite a book of collected articles rather than citing every single article individually. In that case, simply omit the name of individual web pages or posts, and give the URL for the home page of the website or blog. If the website or blog is an ongoing work, you might cite the year it began and the current year, as in the example below:

Lee, Anna (2005–07) *Rat Wars* <www.anysite.com/members/~annalee/ratwars> Accessed: 12 March 2007.

Sometimes you will need to make reference to the website of an organization, a source for which there is no close print equivalent. In this case, the date the organization first made the website available online is really only of historical interest, because they have an ongoing presence online. By contrast, a blog or personal website may only last for a year or two. The date you viewed an organizational website is irrelevant if you are referring to a site that you viewed on multiple occasions. In this case, you can list websites separately from other sources, as you might list newspapers or archive collections you used extensively. You can omit dates entirely, as in the example below:

Organization for Economic Development <www.oecd.org>.

Dealing with page numbers

In many disciplines you are expected to cite a page number when you make reference to a particular sentence or paragraph in a print document so the reader can find it easily. Giving page numbers for web documents presents some difficulties. If the document is in PDF format, where all of the pages are clearly numbered, there's no problem. But a web page that is seven pages long on your printer could easily be five or nine pages long when printed out on another printer with different settings. One way around this problem is to give the total number of pages in the document, citing it as '2 of 7', for example. This gives a clear indication which part of the document the quote appears in, even to someone whose printer is set up differently or who is viewing it through their browser. In some types of print documents, such as parliamentary debates or legal documents, it is established practice for paragraphs to be numbered. You cite the paragraph rather than the page number. Where a web document is numbered by paragraph, you can cite these rather than page numbers. Finally, bearing in mind that the central concern here is to be able to locate the original, one of the most effective ways for a reader to locate a quote in a web page is to view the page on their browser and use 'Find' to locate the quote. This fact renders the citing of web page numbers redundant when a quote is involved.

Citing email messages

These are a lot simpler to cite than web documents, requiring minimal detective work. The author is usually the person who sent the message. If the email address is publicly associated with the message (for example, if it was sent out on a public mailing list or if it is available on a website or in a public archive), you can give the email address in the citation. If not (that is, if it is a private message or one intended for a strictly limited audience), then you should ask permission before you quote it or cite it at all. The date is usually the date it was sent first and the title is the subject heading or an obvious title at the beginning of the message. For email messages, the equivalent of 'site' is the discussion list or mailing list that the message came from – if it came from a list. If it is unclear from the name of the list that it is an email list, put the mailing address for the list after its name, just to make this clear. If it came directly to you from an individual, then 'site' is irrelevant. In the case of such private messages you should include the name of the person the message was sent to. If an email is archived on the web, you can also give the URL to allow people to locate the original easily.

Below are two different ways to cite the same imaginary email message, depending on whether it was a private message or one sent to a discussion list.

Message sent to the Quitsmoking-L discussion list

Mulcahy, Dara (2007) <dara@mulcahynet.ie> 'Giving up cigarettes in Belfast', *Quitsmoking-L*. 28 December 2007 <www.quitsmoking.ie/list/message 432.html>.

Private email message

Mulcahy, Dara (2007) <dara@mulcahynet.ie> 'Giving up cigarettes in Belfast', Email to Niamh Quinn. 28 December 2007.

Citing discussion group posts

You cite these in much the same way that you cite email messages. Author, date and title are all straightforward enough, while the group the message is posted to is the equivalent of the site.

Mulcahy, Dara (2007) <dara@mulcahynet.ie> 'Giving up cigarettes in Belfast', *soc.smoking.ireland*. 28 December 2007.

Citing photographs

Printed photographs often belong to collections and are cited as such. If an online photograph belongs to a wider collection online, include the name of that collection in the citation. If it is not, then simply omit this element. The example below cites a photograph that does belong to a wider collection identified as such by the photographer. Ideally, you should provide a URL that will lead directly to the photograph. If a photograph is embedded in a web page and you can't provide a direct link to it, provide the URL for the page.

Lee, Anna (2007) 'Footprints in grease' [Photograph]. Kitchen scenes
<www.flickr.com/photos/annalee/130794732>.

Exercises

Exercise 1: Classification

Do a quick search on a keyword search engine such as Google, Yahoo, MSNSearch or
Ask.com on a topic that generates controversy and debate. It does not have to be connected to your research topic. You might choose a topic such as 'assisted suicide', or
'insurgency'.

Quickly classify the first five hits and briefly explain why you have classified them in this
way, describing the information that was crucial in making your judgement. If all five
belong to the same category, continue into the next five hits to ensure that your answer
deals with hits from at least two different categories.

Exercise 2: Evaluation

Choose two of the web pages you classified in the first exercise, making sure that they
belong to two different categories.

Evaluate both of them for authority, accuracy, objectivity and currency, according to the
guidelines suggested above.

Which evaluation questions proved most useful in assessing these web pages?

Exercise 3: Citing web pages

Cite the two web pages evaluated in the previous exercise.

Exercise 4: Citing a blog entry

Use a blog search engine such as Google Blog Search or Technorati to identify a blog
entry on a topic that generates controversy and debate.

Cite the entry, and cite the blog the entry was posted to.

Exercise 5: Citing an email received from a list

Cite an email you have received from a mailing list.

Exercise 6: Citing a discussion group message

Search Google Groups or Yahoo Groups to identify a post on a topic that generates controversy and debate.

Cite the post.

Exercise 7: Citing photographs

Cite a photograph you have identified through the image search of a major search engine such as Google, Yahoo, Ask.com or MSNSearch.

Cite a photograph you have identified through a photo-sharing site such as Flickr, Webshots, or Pbase.

Bibliography

Adams, Douglas (1979) *The Hitchhiker's Guide to the Galaxy*. London: Pan Books.

Agre, Philip E. (1996) 'The art of getting help', *Red Rock Eater News*, 8 October 1996. <rre@weber.ucsd.edu>.

Ahrens, Frank (1999) 'The cyber-saga of the "Sunscreen" Song', *The Washington Post*, 18 March 1999 <www.washingtonpost.com/wp-srv/style/features/daily/march99/sunscreen0318.htm>.

Alexander, Janet E. and Tate, Marsha Ann (1999) *Web Wisdom: How to Evaluate and Create Information Quality on the Web*. Mahwah, NJ/London: Lawrence Erlbaum Associates.

Antelman, Kristin (2004) 'Do open-access articles have a greater research impact?', *College & Research Libraries*, 65 (5): 372–382. <eprints.rclis.org/archive/00002309/>.

Basch, Reva (1996) *Secrets of the Super Net Searchers: The Reflections, Revelations, and Hard-Won Wisdom of 35 of the World's Top Internet Researchers*. Wilton, CT: Pemberton Press.

Basch, Reva (1998) *Researching Online for Dummies*. Foster City, CA: IDG Books Worldwide.

BBC News (2005) 'Authors sue Google over book plan', *BBC News*, 21 September 2005 <news.bbc.co.uk/1/hi/business/4266586.stm>

Best, Samuel and Krueger, Brian (2004) *Internet Data Collection*. London: Sage.

Calishain, Tara (1998–2006) *ResearchBuzz* <www.researchbuzz.com>.

Ellis, Judith (1993) *Keeping Archives* (2nd edn). Port Melbourne: Thorpe in association with the Australian Society of Archivists.

Encyclopaedia Britannica (2006) 'Fatally flawed: refuting the recent study on encyclopedic accuracy by the journal *Nature*' [press release], March 2006.

Feeney, Mary (ed.), National Preservation Office (1999) *Digital Culture: Maximising the Nation's Investment*. London: British Library.

Giles, Jim (2005) 'Internet encyclopaedias go head to head', *Nature* 438, 15 December 2005, 900–901.

Grossman, Wendy (1997) *Net.wars*. New York: New York University Press.

Hine, Christine (2000) *Virtual Ethnography*. London: Sage.

Hine, Christine (ed.) (2005) *Virtual Methods: Issues in Social Research on the Internet*. Oxford: Berg.

Hoff, Jens, Horrocks, Ivan and Tops, Pieter (eds) (2000) *Democratic Governance and New Technology: Technologically Mediated Innovations in Political Practice in Western*

Europe. Routledge/ECPR Studies in European Political Science. London/New York: Routledge.

Infopeople (2006) 'Best Search Tools Chart' *Infopeople* <www.infopeople.org/search/chart.html>. (Last updated: 8 March 2006.)

Jacso, Peter (2005) 'As we may search – comparison of major features of the Web of Science, Scopus, and Google Scholar citation-based and citation-enhanced databases', *Current Science*, 89 (9): 1537–1547.

Jones, Steve (ed.) (1998) *Doing Internet Research: Critical Issues and Methods for Examining the Net*. London: Sage.

Jones, Steve and Madden, Mary (2002) *The Internet Goes to College: How Students are Living in the Future with Today's Technology*. Pew Internet and American Life Project <www.pew internet.org/pdfs/PIP_College_Report.pdf>.

Jones, Steve and Johnson-Yale, Camille (2005) 'Professors online: the Internet's impact on college faculty', *First Monday*, 10 (9) <firstmonday.org/issues/issue10_9/jones/index.html>.

Kaye, Barbara K. and Johnson, Thomas J. (1999) 'Research methodology: taming the cyber frontier: techniques for improving online surveys', *Social Science Computer Review*, 17 (3): 323–337.

Kitchin, Rob (1998) *Cyberspace: The World in the Wires*. Chichester: John Wiley.

Kollock, Peter and Smith, Marc (eds) (1999) *Communities in Cyberspace*. London/New York: Routledge.

Mann, Chris and Stewart, Fiona (2000) *Internet Communication and Qualitative Research: A Handbook for Researching Online*. London: Sage.

Mintz, Anne (ed.) (2002) *Web of Deception: Misinformation on the Internet*. Medford, NJ: CyberAge Books.

Nesbary, Dale K. (2000) *Survey Research and the World Wide Web*. Boston, MA: Allyn and Bacon.

Notess, Greg (1999–2006) *Search Engine Showdown* <searchengineshowdown.com>.

Pfaffenberger, Bryan (1997) *Official Microsoft Internet Explorer 4 Book*. Redmond, WA: Microsoft Press.

Sondermann, T.J. (2004–06) *On Google Scholar* <schoogle.blogspot.com>.

Sullivan, Danny (ed.) (1997–2006) *Search Engine Watch* <www.searchenginewatch.com>.

Tennant, Roy (ed.) (1990–2006) *Current Cites* <lists.webjunction.org/currentcites>.

University of California, Berkeley, Library (2005) 'Finding information on the Internet: a tutorial' <www.lib.berkeley.edu/TeachingLib/Guides/Internet/FindInfo.html>. (Last updated: 31 August 2005.)

Walker, Janice R. and Taylor, Todd (1998) *The Columbia Guide to Online Style*. New York: Columbia University Press.

Wikinews (2006) 'Congressional staff actions prompt Wikipedia investigation' <en.wikinews.org/wiki/Congressional_staff_actions_prompt_Wikipedia_investigation> 30 January 2006. (Last updated: 9 February 2006.)

Wyatt, Edward (2005) 'Writers sue Google, accusing it of copyright violation', *New York Times*, 21 September 2005.

Index